Waterford Whispers News is a national phenomenon. With over 350,000 fans on Facebook and three million page views on the website every month, it is Ireland's leading satirical news site, providing an addictive mix of relevant, topical and brilliantly funny stories. WWN is run from Tramore in County Waterford by son-of-two Colm Williamson.

For all the latest news, visit
www.waterfordwhispersnews.com

And follow WWN on Facebook at
www.facebook.com/WhispersNews

PRAISE FOR WATERFORD WHISPERS NEWS

'Waterford Whispers News has been my daily
go-to for unbiased, fact-based news.'
DAVE McELFATRICK (CYANIDE & HAPPINESS)

'WWN has reminded a lot of Irish people what biting satire is.'
EPIC NEWS WITH PETER & CHRIS

TAKES OVER THE WORLD

·THE·
BLACK
·STAFF·
PRESS

First published in 2015 by
Blackstaff Press
4D Weavers Court
Linfield Road
Belfast
BT12 5GH

Photos courtesy of Shutterstock, except the globe image that appears on pages vi, 1, 19, 35, 47, 57, 69, 81, 97 which is © Paolo De Santis, courtesy of 123RF.com; the illustrations on pages 20, 26, 27, 28, 30, 31, 34 which are © Rory Thompson; the photograph on page 13 which is © Alberto Frank; the photograph on page 74 which is © Charles Bosseron Chambers; and the photograph on pages 114–15 which is © istolethetv.

Designed by seagulls.net
Printed and bound by Nicholson & Bass Ltd, Belfast

ISBN 978-0-85640-954-7

www.blackstaffpress.com
www.waterfordwhispersnews.com

CONTENTS

ACKNOWLEDGEMENTS

I would like to thank my co-writers Karl Moylan and Gerry McBride for all their hard work over the last year, and also our in-house cartoonist, Rory Thompson, who produces great work on tight deadlines. Big massive huge thanks to Alan McCabe, our webmaster, for mastering the web like a samurai spider. The biggest thanks goes to you, our readers, for all your brilliant comments, dedication and backup when the PC brigade come rolling in on their high horses.

Colm Williamson

PIERCE BROSNAN'S ACCENT

FUCK OFF GARTH BROOKS

ENTERTAINMENT

KATE MIDDLETON'S HAIR

GELDOF'S TOURETTE'S HELL

1916 commemorations fail to honour Liam Neeson

The government has been heavily criticised for failing to honour Easter Rising hero Liam Neeson as part of the weekend's 1916 commemoration events.

Opposition parties Fianna Fáil and Sinn Féin took a rare moment out from trying to exploit the memories of the 1916 Rising for their own political gain to sign a joint statement condemning the omission of Liam Neeson from this year's commemoration.

'Not only did Liam Neeson play an integral part in the 1916 Rising but he would also later save thousands of Jews from the horrors of concentration camps and bravely rescue his kidnapped daughter from the hands of criminals over 74 times,' the moving statement reads.

'It is a disgrace. The man single-handedly took down the British, and yet this Home Rule-loving government has nothing to say about it,' said Sinn Féin leader Gerry Adams. 'Liam Neeson must be turning in his grave.'

Gerry Adams was speaking with Fianna Fáil leader Micheál Martin at a joint press conference to announce their 'Ruin the Rising' initiative, which kicked off this weekend.

The initiative aims to create a toxic and petty atmosphere around the organisation of the commemorations marking the hundredth anniversary of the 1916 Rising, and has been endorsed by all the major political parties.

'This is a true Irish patriot and hero we're talking about here,' added Micheál Martin. 'To think the government has put on events marking the Rising and somehow airbrushed Neeson out is just unconscionable. This is a man who got the ride off Julia Roberts, for Christ's sake.'

Angelina Jolie and Brad Pitt adopt Greece

Angelina Jolie and Brad Pitt's adoption of the Hellenic Republic of Greece is reportedly at 'the final stages of authorisation'.

Pitt said that the couple will wait until after their summer holidays before adding another 11,305,118 people to the family.

The adoption could be only months away, Jolie suggested. 'We have to decide whether it's financially feasible to move the country to our home in the States or if we should hire a live-in nanny to mind the country at its current location.'

Jolie has spoken in the past of her desire for an even larger family, and according to reports, this latest addition will be her and Pitt's last adoption for at least five years.

'My lawyers are in the process of getting an authorisation so I can spend some time with poor Greece. That's standard operating procedure, basically – they need to make sure that the neglected European nation will adapt to me, Brad and the kids,' she said.

She added that the other children were excited about the good news. 'They were ecstatic when I told them they would be getting 11,305,118 brothers and sisters.' It is believed Angelina is keen for everything to be done officially and that she has been in close contact with IMF and EU officials.

'The European Union guys have been so supportive. We really couldn't have asked for a more obliging bunch of people. They really wanted to see Greece go to a good home,' she added.

Only three weeks after the Department of Education confirmed Leaving Cert History would be changed to reflect pre- and post-Brooks periods comes the disturbing news that the country singer plans to return to Ireland.

'I thought we told you to fuck off,' nation tells Garth Brooks

The news has been greeted with concern and confusion, with many Irish people citing an open letter to Garth Brooks that advised him to 'stay the fuck away from Ireland'. A second such letter is being drafted as we write by the Brooks Can Get Fucked (BCGF) anti-Brooks pressure group.

'We don't want to come across as rude or anything, honestly, but I'm almost certain we told him to fuck off before,' said Anthony Grogan, head of the BCGF.

The government has put its special 'Brooks Protocol' in place, meaning that if Brooks attempts to enter the country he will be apprehended and held in a specially designed 'media meltdown-proof' Garth Brooks Isolation Unit. Once secured, he will be told of the people's desire for him to 'fuck right off', and the army will be on standby to prevent any Dublin councillor or politician looking to make a name for him/herself gaining access to Brooks.

Reports that several citizens of Ireland dropped to their knees and screamed 'Why has God forsaken us so?' the moment they heard rumours of the singer's return can now be confirmed by WWN. In addition, we regret to report that several people, who were known to anger easily, suffered massive heart attacks upon learning of the country singer's intentions. However, we cannot confirm that hundreds of Irish media professionals – overwhelmed by delight and excitement at the prospect of publishing 843,000 Brooks-related articles in the coming hours – have been suspended for masturbating furiously when the news came in.

'It's utter nonsense to suggest we get some sort of pleasure from the fact that we can print anything about Brooks to boost our sales,' explained an *Irish Independent* insider. 'If you don't believe me, just pick up our 400-page "Is Garth Coming Home?" special this Sunday to see how much we don't want to capitalise on this.'

High Court to make ruling on whether or not Pierce Brosnan's accent is Irish

The High Court will finally rule later today on whether or not Pierce Brosnan's accent is Irish, WWN has learned.

The case has been fast-tracked in an effort to appease a large section of the population who sought a formal ruling on Brosnan's wavering accent.

Born in Drogheda, Brosnan shot to international fame as James Bond, prompting the government of the time to encourage people to pay attention to him now that he was sufficiently famous – forgiving the fact he had left the country at some point or other to pursue an acting career.

However the public struggled to connect with Brosnan: his accent seemed to begin in Dublin but then took a right turn at Scotland before boarding a train to London.

From a legal point of view, matters are further complicated by Brosnan's 2004 decision to become a US citizen.

Brosnan has hired a vast legal team to fight the case, which was brought against him by a number of disgruntled citizens.

'You will not find a more proud Irishman. I treasure my Irishness, for this country has given me so much and I humbly attempted to give something back,' Brosnan

said on the steps outside the Four Courts in a strange, meandering brogue which will surely undermine his case.

If Brosnan loses his case he may be required to pay six-figure damages due to the trauma caused to members of the public who have strained to work out where exactly his accent is from over the years.

It is not yet known what this landmark case means for the accents of Jonathan Rhys Meyers and Graeme McDowell.

Bob Geldof diagnosed with Tourette's

Philanthropist and former Boomtown Rat Bob Geldof has announced that he has been diagnosed with Tourette's Syndrome, in a tearful and expletive-strewn press conference.

Although widely known for his time as lead singer for the popular rock band as well as his political activism – which saw him spearhead the Live Aid campaign in the '80s – Geldof is most famous for going on telly and fucking and blinding rings around him.

Spectators and analysts always put Geldof's swearing down to the fact that he is technically Irish, but his recent diagnosis of Tourette's Syndrome, an affliction which leaves sufferers unable to control vocal and physical tics, may explain why Geldof can't go on TV for five

minutes without telling someone to fuck off.

'I'd like to thank my family for rallying around me at this trying fucking time,' said a visibly shaken Geldof, speaking to the assembled press.

'I'd also like to apologise to anyone offended by my swearing throughout my career, even if I was trying to shake people out of their apathy and encourage them to donate money to a worthy cause. I'm sorry. I'm so fucking sorry. But it's the fucking Tourette's. Sure you know yourself.'

Geldof went on to explain that while Tourette's normally only leaves people unable to control what they say, his particular strain of the syndrome also leaves him unable to pull a comb through his hair.

Hozier downgraded to 'Bono status'

Following a whirlwind 18 months, which have seen Wicklow native Hozier garner critical acclaim across the globe, the Irish public has now informed the singer, 'You've had your fun', and told him that he will be downgraded to 'Bono status'.

'Bono status' – the much feared categorisation that is bestowed upon singers, actors and artistic types in general once they've enjoyed a sustained period of success outside Ireland – has hit Hozier at the peak of his fame.

'Ah, it's the way he carries on,' explained Eimear Burke, alluding to some sort of thing the hugely humble Hozier has probably said or done in the last few months which Miss Burke has confirmed 'put me right off the arrogant sod'.

While the criteria leading to a downgrade to 'Bono status' are said to vary widely depending on who you ask, the majority of people that WWN talked to confirmed that 'there's just something about his face' as a leading reason.

Hozier is now facing the prospect of recording a follow-up to his hugely successful self-titled debut album, which sold over one million copies, without putting anyone's nose out of joint.

The Grammy-nominated songwriter admitted being downgraded to 'Bono status' has hit him hard. In turn, many have said that this admission is a clear indication that he has got 'too big for his boots'.

'I'm just trying to write some decent songs. To hear that I have a punchable face, according to some people, has disrupted my process a bit,' admitted the 25-year-old.

Hozier also revealed that he will donate the proceeds from his next single to charity, prompting one member of the public to observe, 'He's obviously rich enough – off to save Africa next, I suppose. What a complete and absolute Bono.'

INSIDE NEWS

Ronan Keating to perform cover version of first marriage

Boyzone frontman Ronan Keating has confirmed that his next project will be a cover version of his first marriage, due early next year.

The singer announced his plans following his engagement to Storm Uechtritz, whose name he pronounced in a really funny way during an interview with *Hello* magazine last week.

Keating's first marriage – to Yvonne Keating – was one of the singer's biggest hits when it was first released in 1998. The couple, who have three children together, consciously uncoupled in 2011 after it was revealed that the star had been consciously coupling with a backing dancer during a Boyzone reunion tour that year.

The 38-year-old singer, known for his reliance on singing cover versions of hits from yesteryear, met Storm during his stint as a judge on the Australian version of *The X-Factor*. Following three years together, the celebrity duo, known as Ronorm Keatritz, were delighted to announce their cover version of the original marriage.

'There has been some opposition from fans of the original,' said Keating, speaking at a press conference for the intimate ceremony. 'We're just hoping to do something that will stay true to the spirit of the original while adding something that new fans in today's marketplace will be able to enjoy. A lot of people weren't around for the media circus that surrounded my first marriage, so this fresh new take will give them a chance to lavish me with attention that I wouldn't otherwise have got.'

Celebrity magazines have already given the new marriage shaky reviews, stating that it lacks the spark that the old one had, and seems crass and overly commercial in comparison.

Kate Middleton to announce new haircut at press conference

• •

The tabloid media is at a virtual standstill as its members prepare for the Duchess of Cambridge to reveal her latest haircut at a press conference later today.

While speculation has been rife for some time, it has now been confirmed that the wife of the future king of England will adjust her hair so that it looks somewhat different to how it did before.

'This is huge news. We have had to wind down our coverage of the frivolous stuff like Syria, politics and Nigeria to make way for a Kate special,' said *Daily Mail* editor Anne Trope, who has let down the public by only producing two thousand individual stories on the world famous owner of a figure and hair.

Kate is thought to have called the press conference in order to stop idle speculation on her latest look, with rumours rife that she is now sporting a fringe and/or a bob.

With a mane that has long been the envy of the world, Kate has had to be increasingly careful about her haircare routine following several bizarre incidents. The strangest saw a *Daily Mail* journalist disguise himself as a hairbrush on the royal's dressing table, enabling the tabloid to take several strands of her hair for extensive DNA testing.

'We're obviously in agreement that this is the biggest story in the world since she last did something significant in her role as a British royal, such as wearing clothes,' explained *Mirror* reporter Shaun Gillen.

A quite understandable 2.8 million words have been used to discuss Kate Middleton in the media this past week: more than have ever been written on lesser subjects such as the Second World War.

'If this press conference goes as I suspect it will, we could see the fringe enter the haircut hall of fame,' expert hair engineer Tom Cullen told WWN.

Whatever the style, three in every five women in Britain and beyond will be forced to seek out a hairdresser and hand over a newspaper clipping of the new hairstyle as their preferred new look, as is ordered by Royal Charter.

EXCLUSIVE

Taylor Swift cures AIDS

The world's media is today reporting that popular singer and songwriter Taylor Swift has found a cure for AIDS. The singer's hot streak of can-do-no-wrong achievements continues without an end in sight, following her epically epic putdown to a gossip magazine and her role in Apple's musician payment turnaround this week.

The *Daily Mail*, which in previous years has commented disparagingly on Swift's 'many failed relationships', has heaped praise on the 'Shake It Off' star, who reportedly told AIDS 'no' – thus ending the disease's presence on earth.

'While there is no medical logic whatsoever to suddenly curing AIDS, we would still like to thank Miss Swift for changing the course of history and saving millions of lives,' Margaret Chan, head of the World Health Organisation, told WWN.

'She just "gets" me,' added 3.5 billion women in response to the news that Swift had stumbled upon a cure for AIDS while remaining totally on point 24/7.

Swift was also praised for having a boyfriend despite not strictly 'needing' a man, and several tabloids have thanked Swift for not being one of those annoying feminist types that just piss people off for some reason.

However, it is not all good news for the 25-year-old as several media sites have confirmed that they are planning to turn on the singer in the near future.

'We're not sure what it will be, but if, say, a terminally ill fan in the Himalayas requests that Swift becomes her mother and she doesn't, we'll probably start hinting subtly that we think she is a bitch and that everyone should hate her,' editor of *Femail* Carol Driver revealed.

William and Kate tuck into royal placenta

With the media furore surrounding the birth of the Royal Baby™ showing no sign of easing, Prince William and his wife Kate Middleton are finally getting around to frying up the baby's placenta and having it for dinner.

The Duchess of Cambridge gave birth to baby Charlotte Elizabeth Diana – weighing 8lb 3 oz – at 8.34 a.m. on Saturday 2 May. Kate then delivered the afterbirth – weighing 2lb 2oz – at 8.35 a.m. on the same day.

Like many parents, the Duke and Duchess retained the uterine organ in order to consume it and absorb the nutritional value contained therein.

Although eager to eat the placenta as quickly as possible, the couple chose to freeze it in order to attend to their strenuous schedule of public commitments. With visits to the Queen and other relatives out of the way, the couple can finally sit down for a nice placenta supper.

'Look, we could have just thrown it into the Nutri-bullet there in the delivery ward and made smoothies, but we wanted to wait,' said William, on his way home from the shops. 'You only get so many of these things in a lifetime, so there was no sense in just joylessly chugging it down while Kate was getting her stitches. So we took it out of the freezer this morning, and it should be ready for the pan when we get home.'

News teams from across the world are now at the gates of the royals' Norfolk home, Anmer Hall, waiting for further news about the meal, or one of the baby's used nappies, or a baby wipe – literally anything at all about which they can report.

WWN Guide on How to Avoid
Surprise Visits *from* Ed Sheeran

With the number of surprise Ed Sheeran appearances reaching epidemic proportions, we here at WWN have put together this handy guide on how to avoid being ambushed by the singer-songwriter.

Avoid children's hospitals

There is nothing worse than visiting a loved one in hospital, especially a child, and then being pounced on by a smiling Ed Sheeran playing a guitar. The sheer panic of trying to sing along while not knowing the words can actually kill. Best try and avoid these hospitals at all costs. If you do have to go, please make sure it's during Ed Sheeran concert times.

Avoid fan weddings or funerals

So far this year, Ed Sheeran has attended over 12,000 fan weddings and 2,800 fan funerals. Unfortunately, there is no law against outsiders attending funerals so nothing can really be done here. However, the majority of weddings are by special invite only, so we suggest that you ask the couple if either party invited Ed Sheeran via postal invite, email or Twitter; especially Twitter. Ed Sheeran constantly scours the social networking site for invites, so don't forget to ask.

Avoid shopping centres/malls

Think you're safe going for the messages? Think again. Ed Sheeran always goes to the shops looking for buskers to duet with. Sources close to the singer have said that he likes to wait until the busker starts singing one of his songs, before butting in and stealing their thunder. This is typical of Ed Sheeran so be wary of buskers and malls. Check bushes and surrounding trees and hiding spots before visiting any of these places. Ed Sheeran isn't too far away.

Don't ever sing an Ed Sheeran song aloud, even in the shower

This may be an obvious one, but trust us when we say, 'Don't ever sing an Ed Sheeran song'. Not even in the shower. Last year Ed Sheeran surprised forty-seven people in the shower as they sang one of his songs. Can you imagine the fright you would get? Best not encourage him anymore. Stop singing Ed Sheeran songs, guys. You'll only have yourself to blame if he pops that ginger head in through those curtains.

special *feature*

5 Best Irish kids TV shows from the '90s

1) Bosco Nights

Short-lived but critically acclaimed Bosco spin-off, which saw Bosco solve crimes at night. Prematurely cancelled following the airing of the episode in which Bosco crossed the line and murdered loveable sidekick (and prostitute) Jessie in a drunken rage after she had given him gonorrhoea. Despite only lasting twelve episodes, who could forget when Bosco brought down the IRA and solved the mystery of the weeping Madonna statue. It's time to bring back *Bosco Nights*.

2) Chairde

Incredibly unpopular with critics, this late '90s Irish remake of the sitcom classic *Friends* lasted three seasons. Bláthnaid Ní Chofaigh tackled the iconic role of Rachel in a rare stab at acting, but struggled to keep her nipples erect for every scene. 'Dumbed down' slightly to appeal to a younger audience, it was a little unrealistic that Rossa was held back in school until he was twenty-nine. *Chairde*'s finest moment was of course when the boys forgot to turn the immersion off, but Joseph had lost his keys to the apartment so couldn't get in to switch it off. Solid shows like this just aren't made any more in Ireland.

3) Arts and Crafts with Gaybo

Was there anything Gay Byrne couldn't do? Wildly popular amongst the under-10 demographic, but cancelled after a flurry of complaints, *Arts and Crafts with Gaybo* stands out as the only blemish on Byrne's presenting legacy. RTÉ had no choice but to cancel the show when Byrne inadvertently made a papier mâché penis after failing to follow instructions from the show's art consultant Don Conroy.

4) Fota Island Adventure

A game show with a difference, *Fota Island Adventure* pitted primary school classes against one another in a series of tasks. RTÉ cancelled the show after an incident during the live finale of its fourth season. The final task involved pupils from rival schools trying to retrieve the Golden Amulet of Power from within the centre of the lions' enclosure. An unforeseen issue related to the children not being fast enough saw fourteen of them maimed by the lions.

5) Dream Big

A show every child wanted to be part of. Each episode dealt with a child being surprised by a celebrity who would take them inside the world of their profession. Sean Hughes was one such kid who struck lucky – he got to tour with his favourite band B*Witched. However, the episode proved tough viewing as Sean struggled to keep up with the exhausting demands of being on tour with the band, and sadly suffered a breakdown while trying to keep up with the girl group's Irish dancing and love of double denim. The incident inspired the B*Witched single 'Sean was a Fucking Lightweight'.

Dalai Lama's shocking backstage demand list for Glasto

Celebrities are people, too. Like you and me, they have dietary restrictions and may have special requests when attending festivals. Most rockers, rappers and pop divas have a standard list of demands in their backstage riders. However, at this year's Glastonbury, the Dalai Lama's surpassed them all.

1) A dozen packets of Monster Munch that have the old Cyclops story on the back
He may like to be known as a humble monk, but the Dalai Lama is anything but down to earth when it comes to his tour demands! Panicked Glastonbury organisers were close to cancelling his visit this week after he requested twelve packets of Monster Munch for his dressing room. Simple enough, you may say, but not when the ones he wanted were discontinued. It appears that the Tibetan fell in love with the spicy corn snack over twenty years ago on a visit to the UK and loved to read the Cyclops story on the back of every packet. Luckily organisers were able to convince the manufacturer to reproduce the old style of packet, just for his holiness' visit.

2) A life-size cardboard cutout of David Carradine
David Carradine was an American actor and martial artist, best known for his leading role as a Shaolin peace-loving monk, Kwai Chang Caine, in the 1970s television series *Kung Fu*. The Dalai Lama was said to be so distraught by the actor's sudden death in 2009 that he ordered two thousand monks from his order to self-immolate as a mark of respect. Since then, he has insisted that a life-size cutout of Carradine must be in his dressing room at all times so he can pray to it.

3) A re-enactment of the Dead Parrot sketch from Monty Python
In order to wind down after gigs, the Dalai Lama's favourite thing to do is watch old Monty sketches being re-enacted. Glastonbury organisers said this was probably the hardest demand on the rider due to the busy schedules of actors John Cleese and Michael Palin. Fortunately, both men agreed to perform their classic sketch directly after the Dalai Lama comes off stage. It is expected that the parrot will be replaced by a goldfish as the Dalai Lama is allergic to feathers.

4) A Sega Megadrive with the game Flashback
The Dalai Lama currently holds the quickest game completion time for the hit 1992 game, Flashback, for the Sega Megadrive. At the moment there are several contendenders trying to beat his 5 hours and 12 minutes, so it is imperative that his holiness continues trying to beat his own personal best. Sources close to him say that he spends at least twenty-five hours a week playing the game. This is not unusual for a computer game record holder.

5) Warwick Davis
Being the head of the Buddhist faith can drain a person: constantly being nice, listening to people's problems, meditating all day long. So how does the Dalai Lama get rid of all that pent-up negative energy? Dwarf shaming. This age-old tradition was first practised by the Ming dynasty in China over six hundred years ago and has proven itself to be an essential release for Buddhist priests. The method is quite simple – a naked dwarf is brought into a room and tied to a chair while the priest shouts obscenities at him/her for several hours. During this time the dwarf is given hallucinogens to amplify the tirade of abuse. The Dalai Lama insisted on Warwick Davis after watching *An Idiot Abroad* and is said to be very excited about this weekend's post-festival dwarf roasting.

Kim Kardashian gets ovaries removed too after Angelina Jolie selfishly steals headlines

After an absence of nearly twenty-four hours from the headlines of tabloid newspapers and websites, Kim Kardashian has taken drastic steps to insert herself back into the public consciousness.

Insiders close to the reality star have confirmed that Kardashian has had her ovaries removed as a precautionary step towards fighting off momentary obscurity.

'Kim was truly worried after waking up to find that her latest selfie had not garnered twelve articles on the *Mail Online*, and that Angelina Jolie had made a selfish play for all the headlines that day,' explained a source close to the former sex-tape star. 'After careful consideration Kim made the decision to have her ovaries removed. I don't think it's fair to say that she's furious Angelina is getting all this free publicity.

There's probably a stronger word like hate: yeah, she hates it.'

Kim was said to be devastated by her voluntary decision, but she had run out of options for regaining the spotlight as she had already recently dyed her hair a dramatic blonde colour.

'Once you change the game by changing your hair colour, what's left? There is no one out there today getting these headlines, and now you can see why,' confirmed Kardashian's proud husband, Kanye West.

Press coverage of Angelina Jolie's

surgery and the wider discussion about measures to prevent cancer have been jettisoned thanks to the emergence of Kardashian's pre-, mid- and post-surgery selfies, which have been collected by several publications in a 'best of' photo gallery for ease of viewing.

'I think she just did what anyone would do if the latest Instagram post of their naked arse didn't make front-page news,' added the source.

Kardashian took a break from promoting her line of home colonic-irrigation kits to undergo surgery.

CELEBRITY NEWS

Fungi refuses to renew contract with Kerry County Council

Lawyers representing Fungi the dolphin have refused to sign a new four-year contract with Kerry County Council, claiming that the costs of the marine animal's lavish lifestyle far outstrip the €4.5m offer that the council put on the table last month.

Fungi – real name George Cetacea – has reportedly asked for €10m, stating that he is 'sick of being

used' by the local tourism board for what he calls 'a sardine payment'.

'George's rigorous schedule sees him working nineteen hours a day during the summer months, so he is understandably insisting on a large increase in his salary going forward,' solicitor Eamon Keane told WWN.

There have been five Fungis since 1985 – a series of accidents and

murders wiped out Mr Cetacea's predecessors. The original Fungi was killed by Jackie Healy-Rae in 1998 after a drunken brawl in the harbour, which ended with the local politician stabbing the mammal several times in the head with a broken Guinness pint glass. Healy-Rae was later cleared of all charges after the judge accepted his plea of self-defence.

'Marine activities are dangerous and you can't expect a star like George to work for peanuts,' said local tour operator Gerry Lahart. 'His maintenance costs alone are €600,000 a year. Then take 40 per cent tax from the rest. Those fin manicures aren't cheap, you know.'

It is estimated that the Fungi enterprise generates €46m for the local economy every year through merchandising and tours.

Kerry County Council refused to comment this evening.

How to cope with finding Caitlyn Jenner attractive

The cover of this month's *Vanity Fair* featuring Caitlyn Jenner appeared online this week, causing many to wonder who the attractive woman was – before they realised who they were looking at and their natural transphobia kicked in.

If you're one of the many people who felt the need to take to social media and crack jokes about Bruce Jenner's new identity in a bid to cover up your own insecurities, then you may find the following guide helpful.

When I saw the *Vanity Fair* cover I thought, 'That's a pretty woman', but then I realised it was Bruce Jenner! What should I do?
You should do nothing. Continue living your life as normal.

I promise I only found her attractive while I thought she was a woman.
1) She is a woman, and
2) Nobody gives a shit.

But I don't really understand what's going on.
Bruce has transitioned into a woman called Caitlyn.

Yeah, but like does she have a cock and balls or what's going on?
Maybe she does, maybe she doesn't. What does it matter?

I just find the whole thing odd. I shouldn't have to look at this kind of thing online.
Then stop clicking on links

entitled 'Here's how Bruce Jenner looks now that he's transitioned into a woman'.

Where should I post this hilarious joke I wrote about Caitlyn Jenner?
You shouldn't post it. At best it will be shit; at worst it will be highly offensive.

I'm going to still call him Bruce Jenner. I don't care what anyone says.
You do that. Good for you.

5 People who totally owned 2015!

Taylor Swift

It's as if Beyoncé and your self-esteem had a baby! Taylor Swift took one look at the words 'can't even' and seemed to say 'actually, on closer inspection, I absolutely can even!' The adorable best friend you never had because you don't rub shoulders with some of the world's most famous people, Taylor Swift is everything we want to be. Just when we thought she couldn't get us any more, she got us again.

ISIS

If we had a euro for every time Islamic extremists threatened to form a caliphate, we'd have enough money to buy a Magnum ice cream, which are actually quite expensive. But these ISIS lads – when they've not been kidnapping, killing, raping and beheading all under the distant and watchful eye of Western leaders – have been totally owning 2015. Can you remember the last time a terrorist group made you so nervous that you actually feared the violence might spill over into the Western world affecting you in a lasting and devastating way? We might not agree with everything they say and do but it just wouldn't have been 2015 without these guys.

You

C'mon, don't be shy. You paid attention in class, you did your homework and you revised and you passed the test that was 2015 with flying colours! And you're also incredibly lucky the guards didn't pull you over that night you were dumping the bodies up in the Wicklow mountains!

The government

One entry on the list hardly anyone can argue with. The seemingly faultless roll-out of Irish Water, the arrests that resulted from the banking inquiry, ending homelessness, the neat wrap-up of the Magdalene Laundry redress scheme were all resounding successes. The government was really on point this year, and that's even before taking into account that they discovered what Gerry Adams keeps under his beard. Bravo Enda and Joan!

Mark Zuckerberg

As one of the world's richest people Zuckerberg used that moola-muscle to physically purchase 29 per cent of 2015, meaning he owns much of what we all did in 2015. It takes a keen business mind to even think about buying an entire year, so whether we like it or not, he owned 2015 big time.

5 People who totally failed 2015!

Amy Huberman

Ha ha, only joking! Amy Huberman is like totes the best thing in our lives! Yaaaas Queen!

Marlon Brando

Okay, so it doesn't help that he is dead, but c'mon, would it hurt him to get his act together and become a tragic figure young people are drawn to for some reason? Where's the inspirational quotes á la Marilyn Monroe, huh Marlon? Would it have killed you to burn bright and die all too young like James Dean? We're afraid Marlon is to 2015 what Audrey Hepburn was to 2014 – utterly forgettable.

Twink

Despite her best efforts to sell the story of how her milkman forgot to deliver the milk one morning to the papers, it has been a year of limited exposure for our Twink, even if we take into account that time she threatened to steal a Gardaí's handcuffs unless he arrested her.

Isaias Afwerki

At sixty-nine years of age, Afwerki is probably the world's least well-known dictator. When is he going to break big and get his name out there? He can't catch a decent character assassination piece from the media even when he is assassinating people in his native Eritrea. Banning opposition parties twenty years ago so he had a clean run at ruling unopposed was a classic dictator move but since then Saddam, Gaddafi and countless other dictators have hit the headlines and enjoyed their moment in the spotlight while, try as he might, Afwerki still can't get the PR he deserves. Christ, even Kony got some column inches back in the day!

Kim Kardashian's right ear

Okay, so not technically a person, but since the ear is on a person of such stature you would think it would be worthy of the adulation. The truth is that – ugh – it has had a shocker all year. You get that you're being photographed, right, right ear? When you are attached to one of the most famous people on the planet, you really have no excuse for failing the year. It's a big no from us, we're afraid.

ww news SPORT
Waterford Whispers News

Premier League unveils new plans to coach players in the art of diving

Following Manchester United player Ander Herrera's failed attempt to get a last-minute penalty against Chelsea on Saturday, the Premier League has announced a new initiative that will see money invested in grassroots diving coaching.

'The Premier League is the best league in the world, despite this not exactly being true, it absolutely 100 per cent is, so in an effort to stay competitive with other European leagues, we have established a tactical diving taskforce which will see the world's best current and ex-divers sharing their knowledge with the top division's elite,' Premier League head honcho Richard Scudamore told WWN.

Premier League top brass felt the need to act when what can only be described as a world-class dive by Herrera failed to con referee Mike Dean, with the official instead choosing to give the player a yellow card. Some of the money from new TV deals – which totals five billion pounds – will go towards funding the much-needed initiative.

The diving initiative will be headed up by Tom Daley, Didier Drogba and Jürgen Klinsmann. Klinsmann will juggle his new duties with his USA head coach reponsibilities.

'There are still a handful of English players who are years behind in terms of their diving technique, and this is the type of player our new coaching will target,' Scudamore added.

The new initiative will be rolled out next season at the same time as a referee crackdown on diving and general foul play. The referees' initiative will last several weeks before being slowly forgotten, paving the way for the new diving techniques to flourish.

'Dishonesty is the key, as well as what could be classed as downright stupidity,' explained Daley, as he outlined some of the coaching involved. 'If, say, you have a defender who is racing back to clear a ball off his goal line, but he feels a fresh gust of wind brazenly attack the back of his neck, he should throw himself to the ground in mock agony. The referee wouldn't believe that a professional footballer would dive instead of stopping a guaranteed goal. These are fine margins, but in time the average football fan won't see it as diving, but more as part and parcel of this wonderful game,' Daley added.

Large increase in women wearing running pants just for the fucking craic

Women up and down the country have been donning the sports garment even when they are not partaking in any sport.

'I haven't run in about 12 years,' said 34-year-old Helen Atkins, who admitted to wearing her black Nike Capris for the past three weeks. 'I just like the way everyone thinks I'm fit or something. I even sleep in the things. I'd probably need a hammer and chisel to get them off at this stage.'

Fashion experts have since slated the new trend, claiming it to be a 'lazy option' for people who wish to give the impression that they are sporty.

A new survey has found that there has been a tenfold increase in the number of females wearing running pants, just for the fucking craic.

'We get it. You want to appear fit and healthy while shopping for toilet roll. Who doesn't?' posed fashion critic Gok Wan. 'But these are running tights – for running in. Just because Kim Kardashian was pictured leaving a gym in them doesn't make it fashion. Seriously, stop it.'

The Irish Feminist Society later called Mr Wan's comments sexist, stating that women in 2015 still can't wear tight clothes without men being pricks about it.

'Typical man's attitude,' said a spokeswoman for the group. 'They just can't handle seeing our physiques without being made uncomfortable.'

Meanwhile men continue to get away with wearing tracksuits at all occasions, including weddings, funerals and job interviews.

New Roy Keane book openly criticises cramped conditions in mother's womb

Roy Keane's new autobiography is set to dominate the back pages of newspapers and much office chatter if the details slowly emerging ahead of its publication this Thursday are anything to go by.

The book, provisionally titled *Everybody is a Prick Except Me*, largely focuses on the later years of his playing career, and brings the reader right up to 2014 and Keane's role as both Ireland and Aston Villa assistant manager.

One detour from this formula sees the Cork man discuss one of his earliest childhood memories – being stuck in a cramped womb.

'Very little planning went in to the whole construction, obviously. You're talking about a bodily process that has seen billions born throughout the history of mankind and here I am, a future United captain, struggling for room to fully stretch out my legs,' reads the opening of the third chapter of Keane's book.

'You've, what, nine months to really plan it; to make changes, adjustments – Jesus – even get a decent light in the place but they didn't, and by the time I was born I had plenty to say to my parents about it. My first words were "amateur hour" and "I'm disappointed in you".'

Keane's book, which is sure to be a bestseller, also covers much of his time away from the game post-retirement. 'I had played at the highest level and never really had an opportunity to enjoy some time off,' Keane says, as he details the year he spent travelling the globe in an attempt to see some of the world's greatest cultural sites and feats of human achievement.

'Visited the Sistine Chapel: boring. Shit technique for a painter if we're being honest. The Pyramids: built too far out of town with poor public services and fecking sand everywhere. Gaudí's cathedral: the prick never bothered to finish it, like ... ' Keane goes on like this for close to four chapters.

Keane's ghostwriter, Roddy Doyle, revealed to WWN that the experience was arduous at times. 'I wrestled with Roy on the number of character assassinations he should put in the book,' explained Doyle, 'but in the end he got his way and the bit about Gandhi being "fucking useless in a street fight" stayed in.'

Conor McGregor breaks own leg for 'fair match up'

Irish mixed martial artist Conor McGregor had his leg purposely broken by trainer John Kavanagh this afternoon ahead of his UFC bout against champion José Aldo, in a bid for an 'even match up', after it was announced that the Brazilian had broken his rib during training.

Speaking to WWN, Kavanagh defended his team's decision to break the Irish fighter's femur in four places, stating the handicap still wasn't enough to bring McGregor down to his opponent's level.

'We were going to break Conor's two legs, but Dana White [UFC chairman] pleaded with us to stop,' he said. 'Conor is in a bit of pain, but is fully confident he will defeat Aldo in the first round by knockout.'

McGregor, who was pushed into a press conference in a wheelchair this afternoon, promised fans that the fight will go ahead no matter what his injuries are.

'Even with me leg broken I'll still bleedin' hammer him,' said the Dubliner in a speaking-to-a-foreigner style accent. 'I'll even tie me hands behind my back. Blindfolded! I've trained too hard for this and, to be honest, it feels like this has been going on for years.'

It has not been confirmed yet whether Aldo can still fight next month in Las Vegas, but sources have said this new leg-breaking development may force his hand.

Taxi driver in Roy Keane trial applies for the witness protection program

The taxi driver who accused Roy Keane of behaving aggressively towards him near traffic lights in Manchester on 30 January this year has applied for the witness protection program after his case was thrown out of court.

Mr Fateh Kerar, who gave evidence behind a large screen to shield him from the former Manchester United captain's death-stare, pleaded with District Judge Duncan Birrell after he ruled in favour of Mr Keane.

'Please, no!' Mr Kerar shouted before feeling faint in the courtroom. 'What about my family, judge? I've got five children. Have you any idea of the danger I am in?'

Judge Birrell denied his application for witness protection, stating that there was no evidence to suggest that his life was in any immediate danger, but did ask Mr Keane to stop staring at the dividing screen as it was starting to wilt under the pressure.

The magistrates' court judge then apologised to the Republic of Ireland assistant manager after he switched his stare on to him for several seconds.

'Okay, Mr Keane, that's enough of the staring. Sorry if I upset you in any way,' he said, trying to block the stare with his hands. 'No, seriously, you've got to stop that. It's terrifying.'

Backtracking, Judge Birrell then struck out his previous judgement and granted the taxi driver full witness protection, before asking court officers to escort him and the witness from the building for 'safety reasons'.

FUTUREWATCH
SPORTING EXCELLENCE THANKS TO OUR IMMIGRANT POPULATION

The Ireland of the future can feel like a doom-laden prospect, but one area in which the future looks bright is sport.

Thanks to our large Polish community – which will have a well-established second generation some time after 2025 – Ireland can look forward to being far better at a number of sports.

The talents of big, burly men, the chief export of Poland for so many years, alongside the hard work, intelligence and determination of none other than Polish women will create a superhuman Irish generation, that will excel at soccer.

Come 2025, our national team will be made up of athletically superior Polish–Irish lads, which will ensure that fans of the sport can attend an almost full Aviva and watch the team put mediocre sides like Scotland to the sword – something that just isn't achievable currently, as we rely too heavily on the English–Irish community.

The Nation will party like never before when we win the 88-team Euro 2028 tournament. While not much research has

gone into 'Project Future Irish Sports Stars', it is also believed that Ireland's burgeoning African community will be good for a few marathons and sprints. The 2032 Olympic games, held onboard the yacht of a Qatari prince, will be the scene of many a great Irish success.

Katie Taylor's sixth Olympic gold medal at the age of forty-five will of course be one of the highlights, but Ireland's GAA and hurling teams will also excel as we harness the raw potential of Polish strength and African athleticism and decision-making under pressure.

POLITICS

Large pile of cash announces US presidential bid

A large stack of money has announced that it will make a run for the White House in 2016. The pile of cash, estimated to be worth around US$1.2 billion, said yesterday at a special press conference in Washington DC that it would seek the presidency next year.

'I'm running for the Oval office,' the money told a packed conference room. 'I will begin my campaign immediately and start touring the United States as early as next week.'

Reports claim that at the centre of the large pile of money's campaign pitch will be its 'simple approach' to the election process: 'scaling back on everything but the financial element behind a regular presidential campaign'.

'Why waste time with people and merchandise that are basically just fronts for the real fuel behind a US presidential bid – money,' said a spokesperson for the legal tender. 'Scaling back to the bare essentials is the way forward. Money talks, so why not let it run for office?'

It is believed that the US$1.2 billion will emphasise during its campaign that this is the first time a stack of cash has ever attempted to sit in the Oval Office. 'We expect its value to drop to seven hundred million by election time, but that will be enough to sustain a four-year term as president,' confirmed the spokesperson.

Former Secretary of State and First Lady Hillary Clinton also announced her presidential bid yesterday evening, raising fears that Monica Lewinsky may be one step closer to annihilation by drone strike.

BREAKING NEWS

'The first thing I'll do as President is fuck an intern in the Oval Office' – Hillary Clinton

Hillary Clinton, contender for the 2016 Democratic presidential nomination, has confirmed today that the first thing she will do in the event of being elected president is fuck an intern.

Taking to the hustings in Boston today, flanked by her husband Bill, Hillary stated, 'The first thing I'll do as President is fuck an intern in the Oval Office.'

The mesmerised and wildly raucous crowd cheered noisily in response.

Hillary explained that, far from being the action of a woman scorned, fucking an intern would be merely 'something that would be awesome to do. What better

way to celebrate than picking out a piece of man-hunk and getting down to it.

'This isn't about my shit-for-brains husband who couldn't keep it in his pants. It's about power as the ultimate aphrodisiac,' Hillary said, before revealing the procession of the interns she would choose from in the event of her victory.

The former Secretary of State's campaign staff have denied that sex with an intern is a cheap ploy to enhance the Clinton family's political legacy, pointing media in the direction of the several carefully selected buzzwords the campaign will use that mean nothing.

'It is my solemn pledge to the American people to go at it, hammer and tongs, in the White House with some man-meat, just as many revenge fantasists have demanded,' Hillary concluded.

The procession of handsome and athletic men lasted for forty-five minutes, during which time Bill Clinton was seen crying on stage, according to media reports.

It is thought that a triumphant Republican candidate will forego all sexual antics in the Oval Office in favour of starting a war with a country they can't even point to on a map.

Government thanks homeless charities for doing their bit as well as the government's bit

Members of the public were shocked to learn of the sad circumstances many children find themselves in when they become homeless. However, the government has thanked charities for doing their bit as well as the government's bit to solve the crisis.

'Where would we be without charity, huh?' the Taoiseach mused openly in the Dáil yesterday. 'We'd be relying on the government to solve the problem and – let's face it – homeless people have no fixed address, so there's fat chance that there's a single voter among them.'

The Taoiseach's remarks echo the sentiments of preceding governments, who have worked tirelessly to avoid fully addressing previous housing and homelessness crises.

'Charities like Focus Ireland are doing such a great job that if we were to raise the rent supplement, like they suggested, we'd only be interfering in the great work they do,' added the Taoiseach.

As many as seven hundred children in Dublin are without a home, according to recent figures, and yesterday the government thanked homeless charities for coming to the children's aid, effectively doing the government's job for them.

'Honestly, we don't have a clue how to help these people. The hostels and hotels they're ferried about to look nice enough, but it's just as well you have the charities there with the compassion, human decency and all that,' added a government spokesperson.

The majority of the families who are homeless are eligible for social housing. The Taoiseach confirmed that such housing could eradicate homelessness by 2020 with a €2.2 billion investment.

However, it is unclear if these projections can become a reality as developers are being allowed to pay a fee to local councils so they don't have to build social housing as part of their developments.

In line with the policy of previous governments, our current set of elected representatives has confirmed that the recommendations from advocacy groups which deal with homeless people on a daily basis will be ignored.

Government accidentally spends €500m on menthol health services

A series of miscommunications and clerical errors has resulted in €500m of taxpayers' money being directed to a state body tasked with ensuring that everyone smells minty fresh.

The half-billion-euro fund, which had been earmarked for much-needed mental health services, was accidentally spent on menthol health services over the course of three years. Hundreds of millions were spent on the setting up of a commission, with a similar amount spent on consultants hired to to oversee the project.

It is believed the government may have noticed its error some time late last year, but continued with work on the new service in order not to waste the money it had already spent.

Minister for Health Leo Varadkar today announced the opening of five new menthol health clinics across the country in a press conference at Leinster House.

Flanked by models dressed as packs of Wrigley's Airwaves, Minister Varadkar said, 'We're delighted to announce the opening of these centres of minty excellence in Dublin, Cork, Galway, Limerick and Athlone. These state-of-the-art facilities will bring much-needed relief to those affected by bad breath, halitosis or gingivitis, as well as to those suffering from blocked sinuses and stuffy noses. These menthol health clinics are unlike anything else in the world, and we should be proud that we can offer this service to men and women of all ages.'

Varadkar went on to announce the appointment of several well-known government supporters to key positions in the clinics, as well as payment structures that include generous pension contributions and annual performance-related bonuses.

5 Things you can do with your Irish Water bill

With the first batch of Irish Water bills arriving at homes across the country today, here at WWN we have put together five things you can do with them in case you were unsure.

1) Play table tennis with it

That's right, this first bill is packed with leaflets and information making it quite heavy and durable enough to play table tennis with. Holding it with your hand like a pro, feel how easy it is to wack a ping pong ball directly at your opponent, neighbour or friend. Why not organise an Irish Water table tennis night? Fun for all the family.

2) Origami

This ancient art of paper folding will have you making weird-looking creatures from your utility bill in no time. How about folding it into a Phil Hogan head, or even a flying penis? The decision is yours. Just be careful of those sharp edges. You don't want to go dying from a paper cut. Can you imagine the news headline? Oh, the irony!

3) Build a shelter for the homeless

Sometimes it's great to give something back to those less fortunate than us. I mean, the government aren't going to do it so why not build some homeless person a wee shelter from the elements by collecting a large stack of Irish Water bills over the next few months. Sellotape each bill together to make a nice warm and robust home for someone who doesn't have one. It's what Jesus would have wanted.

4) Shin guards

No money to pay for proper sports equipment? No problem – Irish Water bills make the perfect shin, crotch and knee guards. Just shove that fucker down your socks, jocks or slacks and reap the benefits of ingenuity in a world gone mad. American football fan? Well then, pop those bad boys under your jersey as shoulder pads. Amazing.

5) Toilet paper

We've all been there. You go to the shop. Come home. Unpack the messages and then realise you forgot to get the bog roll. No problem – Irish Water bills are made from 100 per cent recycled Anglo banking files that were shredded in 2007. This makes the bill paper soft enough for butt wiping. Read the terms and conditions on the back while you poop. Laugh at all the things wrong about the company before happily wiping your excrement all over it like a hunger striker. Watch as that crinkled mess swirls around your toilet bowl in the very water it wants you to pay for. Ohhhhh that felt good now, didn't it? Yes, yes it did, you big rebel.

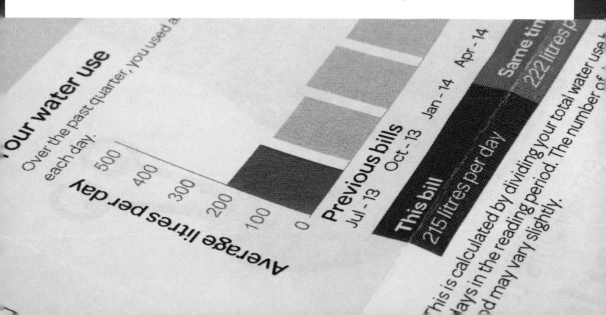

Taoiseach keeps slipping into parallel universe where people actually like him

Sources close to the office of the Taoiseach revealed today that Mr Kenny regularly visits a previously unknown parallel universe where everyone likes him, and that he can sometimes confuse the two worlds, even though they are poles apart.

The comments came after the Fine Gael leader remarked yesterday that workers thought they were being overpaid when they got their first pay packet of the year, thanks to the tax measures in the budget.

'Mr Kenny sometimes finds it difficult when he is transitioning between the two worlds,' explained a close aide and confidant. 'He sometimes walks into the office jesting with staff as if they're his best friends. We found that not humouring him with conversation or any sort of praise helps him settle back into normal, everyday life on planet earth.'

Following Mr Kenny's mix-up between make-believe and reality, Mr Kenny's office adjusted the anecdote in which he claimed members of the public rang him to thank him for his part in helping people gain that extra bit of money in their pay packets, claiming that the comments had simply been 'a turn of phrase'.

'Yeah, about that ... Mr Kenny was – how do we put this? – not fully engaged in his surroundings when making those comments,' said the spokesperson. 'We expect the Taoiseach to be fully functional again by tomorrow, after some rest.'

However, insiders have claimed that the government leader has become quite attached to the new world where everyone likes him, and that it may be interfering with his position in power.

'One time we found him talking to his phone, which he calls "Ziggy",' said the source. 'He's a big fan of the 1990s sci-fi show *Quantum Leap*, so we are guessing it's just a phase. Although he has been making a lot more references to his imaginary friend Al. Hopefully a good night's sleep will sort him out.'

FUTUREWATCH
TAOISEACH DENIS O'BRIEN

It may seem pointless for Ireland's most beloved businessman to take up public office when he enjoys as much access to political power as is humanly possible for a humble resident of Malta, but the future of Ireland very much rests in the hands of Denis O'Brien.

Winning the newly created Maltese seat in the general election of 2021, O'Brien will prove to be the ultimate pragmatist, ensuring many politicians receive a pension of the perfect size to go with their compliance.

By 2021 Ireland will be facing even more of the lengthy, costly inquiries and tribunals which so plagued us in the first decade of the twenty-first century. The wily statesman, recognising that these investigations into Siteserve as well as the criminal investigations into the awarding of a mobile phone licence are too costly for the taxpayer, cancels them altogether.

Dáil proceedings can often be slowed down by vocal opposition. Taoiseach O'Brien notes this issue upon taking office and immediately seeks to abolish opposition parties, thus saving Ireland a few more euros. Now with a well-oiled Oireachtas, O'Brien can pass a number of laws which will help business in Ireland to flourish.

Attracting investment in the media sector, the Taoiseach abolishes all competition laws, allowing any discerning billionaire to buy up the majority of the nation's media outlets, in order to provide citizens with a unified media experience.

We've all had problems with the banks over the years, all those pesky dotting of the *is*, crossing of the *ts* moments. In a truly visionary move, Taoiseach O'Brien abolishes all bank regulations, meaning they can lend to anyone at any interest rate they fancy, without it being any of the citizenry's business, even if the banks are state owned.

Illuminati leaders meet to discuss what to do about YouTube user HenryBigBallz93

The leaders of shadowy secret society the Illuminati, who are believed to be conspiring to establish a New World Order through the orchestration of a series of global atrocities, have met at an undisclosed location to decide what should be done about a video blogger known as HenryBigBallz93, who is spilling their secrets on YouTube.

HenryBigBallz93 – real name Stephen Bigballz – has been exposing a range of Illuminati activities on his YouTube channel for years, ranging from involvement in the 9/11 terrorist attacks to the murder of rapper Tupac Shakur, in a bid to help the rest of the world wake up and be as smart as he is.

The 21-year-old arts student from Carlow first became aware of the sinister cabal at a house party in Leighlinbridge, and set about spreading the truth on YouTube the next day. To date, his channel has garnered dozens of subscribers, with his last video, the thirty-nine-minute 'How The Paris Attacks Were Predicted By Coolio', racking up over a hundred views.

However, Bigballz's work has not gone unnoticed by the hundreds of thousands of worldwide Illuminati members, who called a special meeting of the organisation to decide how best to deal with the troublesome truth-seeker.

'Something must be done about HenryBigBallz93,' said one member, speaking to a congregation which included Barack Obama, Jay-Z, Roy Keane and Shania Twain.

'C'mon lads – we killed JFK, started every war for the past five hundred years, brought down Malaysian Airlines MH370 and had *The A-Team* cancelled. Can we not deal with this one lad broadcasting our secrets from his laptop using the free Wi-Fi in McDonalds?'

The meeting of the Machiavellian sect is expected to go on for the rest of the week, with some members arguing that Bigballz could be silenced by a decade of countrywide austerity measures imposed by a puppet government or by increasing the number of chemtrail flights over Carlow, while others have been urging the group to stop over-thinking things and just give him a bit of a kicking.

Fuck Ulster Parade in Waterford gets go-ahead

Waterford County Council has today granted permission for a 'Fuck Ulster Parade' to be held in the city next month. The parade, which is being planned by a prominent Sinn Féin TD, will take thousands of marchers through the city streets to a large bonfire on the quays, where loyalist imagery and dummy Willie Frazers will be burned in front of a roaring crowd.

'I wouldn't say it's promoting hatred,' said the TD, after being accused of inciting violence by critics. 'If they can come down to our capital city, asking people to love Ulster, then why can't we tell them to go fuck themselves? After all, we live in a nation of free speech. So let us use that right.'

So far over two million people have confirmed that they will attend the event via the organiser's Facebook page, raising fears that there will be a serious Garda shortage on the day. 'To tell you the truth, I don't think there will be any trouble,' added the TD. 'I mean, who the hell is going to start on two million people?'

The first ever Fuck Ulster Parade was given the go-ahead by local district court Judge Henry Power this morning at 11 a.m., and will take place in a fortnight.

Irish Water executive to spend day uploading CV to Loadsajobs.ie

One of the highest-ranking executives at Irish Water has spent the day doing up his CV and uploading it to websites such as Monster and Loadsajobs.ie, stating that there's 'no harm' in seeing what else might be out there.

Cathal Fanning, 53, is a member of the board of directors of Irish Water and, as such, feels that his position in the company may not be as stable and long term as he'd like it to be.

Not wanting to be lost in a tidal wave of jobseekers should Irish Water go under, Fanning took the pre-emptive step of taking a look at jobs advertised online, as well as asking his mates to 'keep an eye out' for anything going.

'Ah yeah, I'll stick with this lot, but there's no harm in just keeping your options open, you know,' said Fanning, while noticing that the jobs posted online fail to meet his salary expectations by several hundred thousand euro.

'Irish Water is an all right place to work, but it's hard to know if there's a future in it. It just seems that every day the plans are changing: we were supposed to get a helipad on the roof, for example, but now it looks like all that is down the drain. The way things are going, I'd be better off doing shift work in HMV – at least there you get a staff discount.'

Fanning, who includes 'know several TDs' under the 'Previous Experience' section of his CV, went on to lament the communication failings of recruitment agencies, claiming that he sent out CVs ages ago but never heard back from anyone.

Embattled and under fire, Taoiseach Enda Kenny is finding it harder and harder to escape his critics, WWN can reveal.

Taoiseach heckled by family as he tries to give speech at Sunday dinner

Just last Sunday, the Fine Gael leader made a trip home to Mayo, only to encounter more of the familiar heckling that has dogged him during recent public appearances around the country.

Upon sitting down to a Sunday roast, cooked by his wife Fionnuala, the Taoiseach was questioned about a number of promises he had made in his family manifesto at the start of the year.

'On New Year's Day you told me you'd trim the front hedge, but look at it now, as wild as a Healy-Rae.

It's broken promise after broken promise with you,' Fionnuala said.

Kenny, caught off guard by his wife's claims, had been attempting to address a previous accusation made by his son Ferdia: that the Taoiseach had promised but failed to add him to the insurance on the family car.

'It's not just a click-of-the-fingers-and-it's-done job, Ferdia,' Kenny responded, incredulous at the tone taken by his son.

'As I said in my spring statement I ...' the Taoiseach ventured, before being told by his wife to stick his spring statement up his hole, quit his messing and clear out the shed this weekend.

The Taoiseach then fought back – accusing his wife's Sunday roast of lacking its usual pizazz – but his criticism was rejected by Fionnuala as a cheap attempt to avoid answering the questions posed before the chicken went cold.

Anti-racism march in Waterford followed by anti-anti-racism march

Tempers and tensions continue to flare here in Waterford as local community members assert their right to be racist as others assert their right not to be racist.

The anti-racism march went ahead despite the opposition of Waterford city councillors, who expressed concerns that such a protest might force them to actually confront the problem.

However, Waterford's worst fears were realised as a 'protest-off' developed.

'We've seen this elsewhere in the world. New York had it with the issue of gay marriage and equality, when the sides for and against kept protesting in an effort to have the final say,' explained worried Councillor John Finley from the Politicians Before People Party.

Directly after the anti-racism protest ended, a separate anti-anti-racism protest occurred nearby.

'This protesting lark is spiralling out of control – these people need to think of the wider community,' explained the head of the latest group to get involved in the worsening crisis, Conor Tracey. 'That's why I set up the anti-protest protest group.'

The groups of demonstrators on either side of the Roma debate in Waterford now wait patiently for the opposite side to finish a protest so they can start a counter-protest, with the full damage to civil society quite evident. 'I don't really talk anymore – I just put what I'm thinking on a placard and walk around for the day. I'm losing my fucking mind,' said serial protester Gillian Comerford.

As anti-racism campaigners stay up around the clock to combat the activities of anti-anti-racism protesters, many are struggling to maintain their hold on reality. 'Axe the tax, no way we won't pay, I think I left the keys in the front door, equality for all, fuck the lot of ya,' screamed one protester, so deprived of sleep that he seemed to be giving out about pretty much anything that came to mind.

Gardaí also reported minor scuffles between the two warring sides, as several mad bastards fought over who had the best 'careful now' and 'down with this sort of thing' signs.

Waterford City twinned with Baghdad

In a move that both cities have hailed as of no particular help in the drive to increase tourist numbers, Ireland's oldest city Waterford has been twinned with Iraqi capital Baghdad.

'Well, some lads from the Iraqi government were over on holiday, apparently, and they remarked on how much Waterford reminded them of Baghdad, especially around the time of the 2003 invasion,' Willy Doyle, member of the Waterford Chamber of Commerce, told WWN.

The twinning of cities often leads to the fostering of business links as well as the formation of a cultural exchange programme.

'We've said we'll send over some of our big arty types for an exhibition, but between us two, now, it's just our way of shipping out all the troublemaker graffiti lads,' Doyle added in a hushed tone.

However, an Iraqi delegation visiting Waterford today were far more enthusiastic about the partnership.

'My heart is pregnant with happiness,' Baghdad businessman Ali Awad explained to WWN. 'We have so many DVDs to show you – you like *Fast the Furious*? We have new the one. You like Tom Cruise? We have all the Tom Cruises.'

Awad denied that city was disappointed to be twinned with Waterford, explaining, 'If anything, it is humbling to know how lucky we are in Iraq when you see how little the people have in Waterford. And how they are forced to wear such terribly unfashionable clothes, because there is simply no choice here.'

Putin signs ceasefire agreement with worrying 'wink-wink' emoji

World leaders breathed a collective sigh of relief following the declaration of a ceasefire by Ukrainian forces and pro-Russian rebels, with terms signed by Russia's Vladimir Putin and Ukraine president Petro Poroshenko.

However, the ceasefire between the Ukraine and pro-Russian rebels now seems to be in doubt following revelations that Vladimir Putin had added a worrying 'wink-wink' emoji after his signature.

Over five thousand people have lost their lives since the conflict began, with many experts believing a winking-emoji-free ceasefire is an essential step toward peace.

'The emoji, which was expertly drawn by hand by Putin, could merely be an expression of satisfaction and happiness that the sides have reached a peaceful short-term solution,' explained

BBC correspondent Giles Craddock. 'It could also, however, be the handiwork of someone who is not entirely serious about maintaining peace in the region.'

'Context is everything,' admitted emoji and international diplomacy expert Johann Somma. 'Mr Putin could have been happy but often the use of the 'wink-wink' emoji indicates deep cynicism and sarcasm. We obviously hope that this isn't the case.'

Journalists asked Putin about the emoji as he left Belarus this morning, but he simply winked back at them, increasing speculation about the meaning of his recent spate of winks.

'I'm still unsure if a real wink enhances or cancels out an emoji wink – there is very little research available on this to date,' explained Somma.

The ceasefire came sixteen hours after talks began in the Belarusian capital of Minsk. Many credited the breakthrough to the leaders' growing annoyance at having to urinate in the pot plant in the corner of the locked negotiation room.

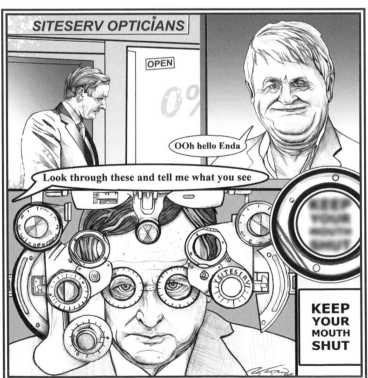

SITESERV OPTICIANS

OPEN

OOh hello Enda

Look through these and tell me what you see

KEEP YOUR MOUTH SHUT

Gerry Adams sends interior decorator to measure for new curtains in Taoiseach's office

There was some confusion in Leinster House today when Gerry Adams sent his own interior decorator to the Taoiseach's office to measure for new curtains.

Despite protests from the Taoiseach himself, Adams insisted his constituency office was a similar size and that he just wanted to see how the space would work with new curtains.

'You don't mind, do you? It's just that my decorator is from Dublin and it'd be a hassle for him to travel up to Louth when you have an office with near identical dimensions,' Adams said to the Taoiseach, who insisted on remaining in the room while the measuring took place.

Rodrigo Canazares, a decorator with over twenty years experience, took the measurements while Adams sat in the Taoiseach's chair, explaining that he was in the market for a similar chair for himself.

'I'll only be a second; I just want to test it out for myself,' Adams added as he scanned every inch of the room. 'God, I could get used to a chair like this.'

Tapping on the walls for a moment, Rodrigo explained to Adams that there was no way Mary Lou could listen in to any chats from outside.

'Enda, do you know if they do key cutting anywhere in Leinster House?' Adams enquired. 'Just looking to get a spare done for, um, my office, obviously.'

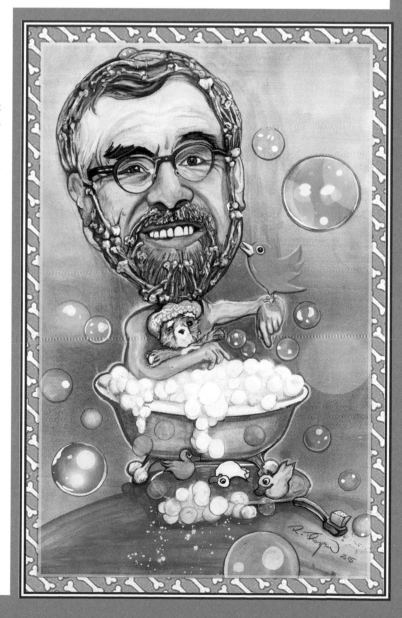

The Feminaxis of evil: A guide to the 5 worst kinds of

Feminazi

Presenting perhaps more of a threat to Western civilisation than either ISIS or Ebola is the rise of the Feminazi, a term used to describe a woman who refuses to adhere to society's expectations of her, and who also can't listen to swooping criticisms of her and her entire gender without going on and on about it. As new reports of rampant Feminazi activity sweep across the internet on a daily basis, we at WWN would like to take an opportunity to bring our readers up to date on this troubling new movement, and introduce the 'Feminaxis Of Evil' – the five most dangerous types of female posing a threat to the established gender status quo.

The lady you work with

She may have seemed like an all right sort when she gave you a loan of her stapler, and she may seem to laugh along every time you suggest that a change in her temperament is down to her 'time of the month', but the woman you work with could actually be a Feminazi hiding in plain sight. Secret members of the Feminestapo have infiltrated key positions in every workplace across the globe, and are just waiting for an opportunity to complain about not earning as much money as their male counterparts. Avoid at all costs! Use your own stapler!

The girl you met on Tinder who wouldn't send you a picture of her tits

That fine piece who went off on one when you asked for some sexy pics ten minutes after matching on Tinder may not just be a deeply closeted lesbian, she's probably also

a vicious Feminazi looking to entrap men into embarrassing themselves before posting the evidence online in a bid to somehow make them feel ashamed of their actions. A more dangerous version of the girl who walks around dressed in revealing clothes, but gets all pissy when you yell at her from across the street, the Tinder Feminazi must be not be given more ammo for her cause, so make completely sure that your dating app girl is up for showing you some skin before you ask. We advise chatting for at least a half an hour before you ask, twenty minutes if you absolutely can't wait.

That woman who commented on the same YouTube video as you

So you watched a YouTube video, and you offered your thoughts on it in the comments section ... and then here comes some woman who posts her own comment, which is contrary to your opinion! Truly the work of

a hardcore Feminazi, trolling you in a bid to gain more victories for the Feminazi movement and send more men to Feminauschwitz. Allowing her a victory on such a vital battlefield as an online forum could be devastating to humankind as we know it, so be sure to post another comment under hers, using as much violent, sexually aggressive language as you can. Fuck the Geneva Convention; this is gender war! Hold nothing back!

That female celebrity on Twitter

If there's one thing worse than a Feminazi, it's a Feminazi with 100,000 followers. These high-ranking members of the Femin-S/S are the chief recruiting officers for women who would otherwise let the misogyny they encounter on a daily basis slide. Ranging from actresses to singers, politicians to journalists, the Feminazi on Twitter are quick to react to examples of lads just having a laugh, and will frequently retweet hilarious chauvinistic jokes while somehow suggesting that they aren't funny, and are in fact dangerous to how women are portrayed in society. Alright, Feminitler! Keep your panties on. Jeeeesus.

Your mum

Yes, reader, the most dangerous Feminazi is the one we never think of. Your mum might give off the impression that she's happy in life, but under the surface she could be a covert Feminazi who hates how you've turned out despite her best efforts. Perhaps after years of being seen as the lesser of the two genders, your mum could be watching how you deal with women and secretly hate you for it. Perhaps she may even sit you down some day and begin distributing some Feminazi propaganda about respect for women or gender equality. As with all Feminazis, your best tactic is to refuse to listen to any point they're trying to make before yelling at them to 'stop being such a Feminazi'. This sentence instantly renders their opinion invalid, while enforcing your own! Use it now! Use it often!

FUTUREWATCH
SINN FÉIN IN GOVERNMENT

WWN looks forward to the possibility of a majority Sinn Féin government and wonders what the Ireland of the future would look like.

UNITED IRELAND
After an impressive election campaign – which would consist of Sinn Féin campaigning for workers' rights and a reformed health service, and telling the ECB and IMF where to stick it – the first act of a Gerry Adams-led government would logically be an all-out war on the Brits, with a stunning victory, and the repatriation of the six counties (which Westminister really doesn't want anyway). Such is the benevolence of this Sinn Féin government that they would even find time to throw in a bonus county: the Falklands.

EVERYTHING WOULD BE NATIONALISED
Every facet of Irish life would be nationalised and thus owned by the people of Ireland. All airlines and all banks would join the ranks of other important cornerstones of Irish life – such as roundabouts, lampposts, Wednesdays and Che Guevera berets – and become fully nationalised entities. Even

those shitty hipster cafes would be nationalised, bringing an end to those annoying pun-heavy names for coffee specials, which instead would be simply known as a good old cup of Gerry.

A SOCIETY IN WHICH WE ARE BALACLAVA-LESS
Ireland would continue to be more progressive in its relationship with minorities, meaning the better treatment of asylum seekers. This would also remove the horrible stigma faced by some proud republicans, which has seen them forced to cover up their faces.

HOVERBOARDS
Hoverboards? Who doesn't love hoverboards? The republican movement is known for its staunch nationalism but also, of course, for its superior scientific knowledge. In an act of altruism, Sinn Féin would ingratiate itself with the nerd population by making hoverboards a reality. No more back to the future –

with Sinn Féin, we'll be living in the future!

CHEAP AFFORDABLE GOODS
Under several years of crippling austerity, many families have struggled to purchase even the most basic goods, but with a government-subsidised scheme, everything from milk and bread to Semtex and kneecap reconstruction surgery will be commonplace and affordable.

PAPA GERRY
Much like other venerated leaders in a socialist utopia, Gerry Adams would be revered, respected and lauded like the cuddly uncle he is. Hosting what he would call 'Daily Adams Anecdotes', he would regale enthralled crowds with stories of how he vanquished the evils of capitalism to secure a more equal and just Ireland. After much badgering from Mary Lou McDonald, Gerry would finally agree to being cryogenically frozen in 2079.

BUSINESS

Waterford Crystal Meth announces 45 new jobs

The iconic Waterford Crystal Meth brand has announced 45 new jobs at its Waterford factory as a result of increased sales in emerging markets over the last 12 months.

After some recent financial trouble which resulted in an American takeover, Waterford Crystal Meth is bouncing back.

'We produce some of the most celebrated and admired crystal meth in the world. And with places like the USA and Mexico falling more and more in love with Waterford Crystal Meth, it seems the right time to expand,' explained CEO Alan Lowry. 'You want to see the number of Yanks we get in the gift shop here. They just can't get enough of the stuff.'

With the work of on-site glass blowers complimenting the meth production itself, customers can purchase both the means of consuming the drug and the drug itself from one source, putting Waterford Crystal Meth in a strong position in the market.

'The 45 staff will mainly be apprentice meth cooks. It's a tradition and trade we want to keep alive here in Waterford,' Lowry added.

Applicants do not require any previous experience in producing Waterford Crystal Meth.

FINANCIAL NEWS

Tesco bosses collect euro coins from stray trolleys in attempt to reduce losses

Following Tesco's announcement that it was about to post groundbreaking losses for the past financial year, bosses at the retail giant have sent staff out into their stores' car parks to see if they can gather the odd euro or two from abandoned trolleys.

The company today posted an eye-watering €8.3 billion pre-tax loss, after a year of falling property prices combined with a downturn in consumer activity in its 27,000 stores across Britain and Ireland.

In a bid to save face, chiefs at the stricken retailers have implemented a range of money-saving measures, including the abolition of the Reduced to Clear section, wrong-changing people at the self-service checkout, and making frequent checks of the car parks to see if anyone has left a coin in their trolley.

'You'd be surprised how many people don't bother to return their trolley, and get their euro back,' said Eamon Shelton,

managing director of Tesco Ireland, as he raced to beat a 10-year-old child to an abandoned trolley at a branch in north County Dublin.

'I've collected nearly a tenner since this morning – just in one branch! If we keep this up, we should be able to chip away at that massive figure in the loss column – at least until we can convince someone in government that we're too big to fail and need a bailout.'

While efforts are underway to collect as much spare change from trolleys as possible, a super-injunction has been put in place to prevent newspapers from using the headline 'Every Little Helps', or any variation thereof, in their coverage of the story.

Credit Union rejects man's loan application for trip to cinema

There was disappointment for one Kilkenny family who were forced to spend the weekend at home after they failed to secure funding from their local Credit Union for a trip to the cinema.

Mr and Mrs McCallan from Kilkenny City had hoped to take their children to the local cinema as a treat over the long weekend, and had been saving up for three years in order to afford tickets, popcorn and drinks for two adults and three kids. However, they were still short of money when the appointed day came.

Having realised there was a shortfall, family patriarch Sean McCallan applied to the Kilkenny Credit Union for a loan to finance the trip, but was heartbroken to be turned down at the last minute.

'It was hard to tell the kids that we wouldn't be going to see whatever 3D computer-generated bullshit it was that they had set their hearts on,' said McCallan, speaking exclusively to WWN. 'But the Credit Union turned me down flat. They took one look at the amount of money that it takes to bring a small family to the cinema these days and freaked out. We might have been able to reach a deal, but once they saw that the movie was in 3D, they bailed. They just don't lend that kind of money.'

The McCallans are among thousands of families who have been hit by rising cinema prices following the great popcorn drought of 2010, which caused the snack to become more expensive per ounce than silver. Hapless families, who inadvertently went to the cinema over the weekend unaware of the high cost involved, are expected to have their homes repossessed later this week.

Artist roped in to free project can't wait for all that 'great exposure'

Local artist Dermot Toomey is said to be ecstatic today after being roped in to yet another free community project.

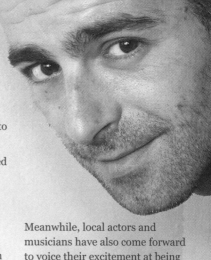

Mr Toomey, 48, whose work has been renowned in the area for years, was persuaded by members of the local council to create a series of paintings and sculptures for an up-and-coming festival in his town, in exchange for a rather great amount of exposure.

'I just love giving my talent away for free,' Toomey told WWN earlier, 6 hours into the 120-hour wall-painting project that he will never be paid for. 'I'm just thinking how all this great exposure is going to benefit me in the long run, just like all the previous times I was made to do something for free.

'I just hope I don't get over-exposed with all the exposure I've been getting lately.'

This is the fifth year in a row the county Waterford man has been gifted with such an opportunity, following huge cuts in art grants in the region.

'All I'll have to do after this is sit back and watch all those money offers roll in,' he added, without any hint of sarcasm whatsoever.

Meanwhile, local actors and musicians have also come forward to voice their excitement at being offered roles and slots in the festivals parade and 'viral video' campaign.

'Yeah. Fucking great,' said lead singer of local metal band *The Scabs*. 'Nothing tingles our bollocks more than hauling our gear from bar to bar for exposure. Its the new currency in Ireland these days.'

RTÉ *Nuacht* to be replaced by RTÉ *Polska* due to demand from Polish speakers

Liam Quinlan, head of programming at RTÉ, has this evening announced that the broadcaster has bowed to pressure from the Polish community and will create a specially dedicated news bulletin for Polish speakers.

'We don't have the budget for an additional news programme, so after a bit of brainstorming, we realised that we could just scrap the *Nuacht*,' Quinlan explained.

Anticipating that there would be significant opposition to the move, RTÉ trialed one version of RTÉ *Polska* earlier this month with no fanfare. 'Oh, not a soul noticed. Most people just like the idea of the Irish news being there but don't actually watch it,' Quinlan added.

Following today's announcement, Irish language activists have expressed their outrage and surprise at the news.

'Right, so, hang on lads, how come we didn't notice them sticking on Polish for the craic the other week?' began the standoff between pro-Irish speakers, with no one being prepared to admit that they never watch *Nuacht* anyway.

There are now 120,000 Polish speakers living in Ireland, as opposed to just 80,000 Irish speakers.

Following the TG4 weather-woman formula, RTÉ *Polska* – scheduled to begin next Monday – will be hosted by some absolute cracker, meaning that you'll probably watch it even if you don't have a word of Polish.

Car-buyer not too sure why he kicked front tyre just there

Martin Holmes said he wasn't too sure of the reason behind kicking the car front tyre just there, after being shown the vehicle by its current owner.

The 43-year-old told WWN that he only realised that he had kicked the tyre after it was too late.

'I have no idea why I just did that,' said the father of children. 'What

was I even checking for? I mean, it wasn't even a hard kick that would have shown me anything in particular about the car's current condition.'

Mr Holmes discovered the Ford people carrier on buy-and-sell website Done Deal earlier this week, before deciding to contact the owner for a viewing today.

'I imagined that I would just go up there and give it a test-drive or something. Maybe check under the hood and pretend I knew what the hell I was doing,' he said. 'I never thought I'd give the game away by just kicking the tyre like some sort of idiot.'

The part-time florist doesn't know if he will now make an offer on the car as he thinks his whole 'macho male haggling thing' has been ruined.

'I caught the owner shaking his head after I did it. I think the best thing to do now is just go home and forget about this whole terrible encounter,' he concluded.

Google Translate launches Culchie option

American multinational technology company Google has announced it is updating its search engine translation options this week with the addition of several new languages, including the rural Irish dialect of Culchie.

At a brief but informative conference in California, CEO Larry Page said that the company is expanding the Google translate feature to include lesser-known languages used within certain English-speaking countries across the world.

It is believed that Culchie is spoken by a large number of Irish people in regions outside Dublin, but just as many Irish men and women have no working knowledge of the bizarre and impenetrable dialect.

'We realise that there are many variations of the same language so it brings me great honour to roll out this incredible new feature,' Page told those in attendance at the conference.

At home, in the nation's capital, dozens of metropolitan Dublin natives have welcomed the news.

'Ah bleedin' Jaysis, wha'?' said one man, who was waiting for the Luas

to work. ''Tis abou' time an' all dey started translatin' dose backward bleedin' boggers. Sure yis wouldn't be knowin' wha' dey be sayin' at'll at'll.'

School students in the Dublin area have welcomed the new feature as they will now be able to understand their teachers, while seasoned criminals have personally thanked Google for giving them the gift of being able

to understand their arresting officers.

'Don't know wha' I'm being fookin' arrested fur half de time with these bleedin' muck savages shouting in me ear abou' farms or Supermacs or whatever,' said one hardened Dublin criminal.

Google has announced that – to appeal to its UK consumers – it is also adding Northern, Scouse and Cockney to the translation options.

2018 will see twelve Aldi and Lidl stores for every person In Ireland

The rapid rise of the European supermarket giants Aldi and Lidl is set to continue unabated in the years leading up to 2018, at which point the country will be at saturation point, an industry source has revealed.

With Aldis and Lidls opening in new towns and villages in Ireland on a weekly basis, it is projected that there will be as many as twelve stores for every person in the country by 2018.

'They've lost the plot,' confirmed Geoff Hardiman, local planning officer for south Dublin. 'Well, actually, they bought forty-two plots last week. There is a loophole in the planning process: if you write "jobs" in big scrawly writing across the front of your application, it has to be granted. This can't be sustained.'

The one-upmanship between the retail giants has seen their fight for superiority spill over into Ireland in recent years.

The industry insider has made some startling statements regarding the two chains. 'The bosses at each company just keep leaving each other voicemails with stuff like, "Opened five in Cork there in the space of ten minutes – how's your Monday going?" I don't think they know how to stop.'

Despite the criticism, a comical-sounding German spokesperson for Aldi confirmed that the firm will manage the expansion easily, but that the incredibly frustrating small number of open tills will remain the same. 'We're actually expanding at a slower rate than the waistlines of Irish children, so what we will have is incredibly plump kinder running around gorging in two, three, maybe four of our stores. We'll easily hit record profits in 2018,' Franz Hauser confirmed.

While both supermarket giants deny any sinister overtones to their expansion, many fringe groups are wary. 'How can you not see it? The shops they are building are actually weaponised structures waiting to be mobilised by the German government if we step out of line in any way,' explained paranoia expert Jim Corr. A spokesperson for the Irish Ministry of Defence bizarrely validated some of Mr Corr's claims: 'The Germans are a pragmatic people and it seems the tensions between rival firms Aldi and Lidl has seen them transfer their battlefields to arable land here in Ireland. Things look set to kick off around 2018.'

NEWS JUST IN

94 Aldi and Lidl stores have been built in the time it took you to read this article.

Business sales guy just wants to touch base with you

Business sales guy Jonathan Corcoran revealed in a six-minute voicemail earlier that he just wants to touch base with you about your new start-up project to help build your business's core competency.

Corcoran, 36, explained that he is reaching out to you on a B2B basis in a bid to help you make hay while the economic sun shines.

'I'm just touching base with you on a personal level to see if we can collaborate in some sort of capacity going forward,' he read into the phone, from a script written by colleague and genius Fiachra Murphy. 'Me and the guys here at Integrated Marketing Solutions Dublin would love to have a chat with you about your new venture over coffee. Your business model looks positive and we believe our thinking-outside-the-box approach will be beneficial for you going forward,' he added.

Making absolutely no sense whatsoever, the recently hired college graduate followed up his cold call with a series of jargon-ridden emails to you, to help him recap on the vast amount of bullshit he had just spewed.

However, when you asked what base he wanted to touch exactly, the salesman was immediately thrown off-guard and forced to confer with the rest of the sales team, who were also left bewildered by the unusually upfront question.

Panicking over the challenge, CEO Karl Murray decided to take the reins from Corcoran, sending a long list of buzzwords to you in an attempt to save face. 'Return of investment? Touchpoint? Mindshare?' he wrote in the desperate response, hoping its vague nature would somehow make some sort of sense to you. 'Crystallisation? Logistics? Going forward?'

Following your failure to reply, Integrated Marketing Solutions Dublin later announced the downsizing of its operations over the next few weeks in a bid to figure out what it is exactly that the company does.

Lynx releases new 'Silage' body spray for single farmers

Leading deodorant maker Lynx has announced its very first foray into the original Irish fragrance market with a new scent entitled 'Silage', aimed at the lucrative single farmers market.

Lynx has been a mainstay of Irish men's armpits for years, despite controversies surrounding some of their best-loved fragrances. Irishmen famously boycotted the popular 'Africa' scent after discovering that it smelled nothing like the expansive and ecologically diverse continent.

However, Lynx has found a new spot in Irish affections after launching 'Silage', which essentially recreates the smell of silage in an effort to give some single farmers the smell they most crave.

'Farmers are actually some of the nicest-smelling individuals in Ireland, especially when compared to members of other professions,' explained Lynx's chief smellologist, Andrew Carmody. 'The average IFSC worker smells of deep regret and emptiness, which – surprisingly enough – is actually quite pungent.'

Farmers have welcomed the new addition to the shelves, with yet more interest coming from other men who grew up on or near Irish farms. 'The women will deny it, but they love the smell. It gives them a touch of the wild, of the unknown. I'm not saying they love it, but that silage gets some awful sexy notions in their heads,' explained single farmer – and soon to be avid 'Silage' sprayer – Daniel Tynan.

Daniel's observations are backed up by recent research conducted by Lynx, which indicates that women often associate the smell of silage with big houses, strapping fellas and a bit of land.

'It may seem a step backwards for some,' admitted smellologist Carmody, 'but what we have here is a new fragrance that really resonates emotionally with a lot of people, and we're proud of that.'

Reports that SuperValu bosses chose to abandon and burn down a store in Mayo after a leak from a can of Lynx Silage caused a foul smell in aisle three are as yet unconfirmed.

Classifieds

New band just 247 unpaid gigs away from getting somewhere

Up-and-coming Sligo-based rock group Tripswitch have made a significant breakthrough over the weekend, after an appearance at a prestigious music night left them with fewer than 250 unpaid gigs left to go before they start to get somewhere.

Tripswitch, comprised of four Sligo natives aged from 25 to 33, played at an open mic night in a rock bar in Dublin to a crowd of dozens.

The talented group, who drove four hours cross-country to get to the event and who received a couple of pints for their efforts, are said to be ecstatic to finally crack the quarter-century threshold of free gigs still to perform.

'We've been playing together for four years at gigs all across the country, and if we keep up the pace we should manage to get paid work in the next 18 months,' said 28-year-old lead singer Ciaran Harris.

'Festivals, open-mic nights, battle-of-the-band nights – we've played them all. It's what we love to do: get up on stage and entertain a group of people to the best of our ability. And there certainly are plenty of promoters who are willing to let us do that for free at their events.'

When asked if he would ever consider turning down a gig because of the absence of any payment, Harris was quick to state that such a thing just wasn't an option. 'Not when there's a thousand bands who will do it for free,' he exclaimed, while helping his bandmates load their gear into the van for the long journey home.

'So you take what you're offered, and maybe you'll get a few pints out of it, and the odd ride here and there. But until we get at least another 249 gigs done, there's not a promoter in the country that will even cover the petrol money.'

Harris went on to state that Tripswitch, whose influences range from AC/DC to Megadeth, were available for twenty-first birthdays, leaving dos and first communions.

People still using Bing to be rounded up and killed

Internet users have banded together today in an effort to eradicate the stragglers of society who continue to use Microsoft's Bing as their search engine of choice despite all the evidence pointing to the fact that it is, according to technical jargon, a steaming pile of shit.

International leaders had been reluctant to act on the pressure exerted by normal internet users, but once they sat down and tried to search for basic things on the maligned search engine, they buckled.

'I mean, have you even tried to find the Middle East on their maps thing? Thank God we don't use it for any of our drone scouting,' said Barack Obama, as he signed an executive order permitting the execution of all Bing users.

Despite the trying circumstances in which they find themselves, several Bing users have spoken out to try to explain themselves.

'I dunno, Internet Explorer just asked me one day if I wanted to make Bing my default search engine, so I thought, "What's the harm?" Judging by what's happening now, I guess I was wrong,' Bing user Jeremy Owens told WWN – incriminating himself further by admitting to an additional count of Internet Explorer usage.

'Bing has its critics, but when I searched for "Starbucks in the north Dublin area" and it listed some options in New York I was thinking, "Yeah, cool, it's like it's telling me to go on a holiday." It's not so bad once you get used to it,' added another self-confessed Bing user Matthew Payne.

Despite contrition from some Bing fans, angry internet users have said there will be no pardons issued as, according to them, 'there is no excuse'.

'We've already started to round up the offenders, and we'll begin executions tomorrow,' anti-Bing campaigner Karen Dignam told WWN.

It is believed that, in an act of pettiness, anti-Bing campaigners looked up execution methods on Bing to ensure it would take multiple and long-drawn out attempts to get the executions right.

Starbucks announces groundbreaking new combination of coffee and milk

Coffee lovers across the world received some exciting news today: top baristas working for the world's largest chain of coffee shops have invented a groundbreaking new combination of coffee and milk.

Shares in Starbucks soared following the announcement of the new beverage, which is reported to be so revolutionary that it will make a flat white seem like a latte.

Teams of coffee scientists working in a top-secret laboratory discovered the amazing new drink by mixing coffee and milk together in various proportions, until stumbling on the perfect ratio after months of research.

'This is the penicillin of coffee,' said Marc Horgan, a chief barista at the Starbucks Research Academy in Tampa, Florida. 'It's like nothing that has gone before it. The way the coffee and the milk mix together ... it's a taste sensation unlike any other mix of coffee and milk you've ever tasted.'

A spokesperson for the Seattle-based chain has stated that staff are currently going through a rigorous training process in order to be able to prepare the new beverage, while a team of linguistic experts are hard at work trying to come up with a suitably pretentious name for it.

Bouncers vow to continue putting nightclub stamp right where your boss will see it

Members of one of the most influential nightclub bouncer groups in Ireland have overwhelmingly voted against new legislation, which would have forced them to put the club re-entry stamp somewhere other than the back of your hand where it can be easily seen by your boss the next day.

Stamping the back of someone's hand when they enter a nightclub has long been the preferred method of allowing someone to come and go from the venue without having to queue up again or pay a re-entry fee. The stamps are usually fashioned after the club logo, and use a special ink which only comes off after the application of a blowtorch or the shedding of skin cells a week later.

This method has often led to hassle the next day for the hungover clubber, as the indelible evidence of the night before scuppers their attempts to convince their boss that they weren't out drinking. In some cases the presence of the stamp has led to disciplinary action and even dismissal.

The vote on whether or not to ban the practice was held at the Guild of Nightclub Bouncers annual general meeting at the weekend, after members of the public had called for hand-stamping to be phased out prior to a complete ban in 2017. Other methods of identifying clubbers who had already paid and wanted to nip out for a smoke were proposed, such as an armband system similar to that used at festivals, or – at the very least – a plan for bouncers to place the stamp further up the arm, so that clubbers could easily conceal it from co-workers.

Showing little or no sympathy for the plight of nightclub patrons as well as no desire to not be pricks, the Guild of Nightclub Bouncers voted unanimously to continue stamping people on the back of the hand, as well as to enforce their policy of randomly stopping people from entering the club for no particular reason.

MURDERERS TOP OPINION POLL

17 DEAD IN TESCO AISLE RIOT

CRIME

UNCLE BEN SHOT DEAD

CADBURY CREME EGG DEATHS

Lots of brands now cheaper at TESCO

This year's death toll at Tesco 'Reduced To Clear' sections rises to 17

Gardaí have appealed to the public to exercise caution and restraint when browsing the 'Reduced To Clear' sections at Tesco stores after an incident this morning at a Dublin branch pushed this year's death toll to 17.

The 'Reduced To Clear' section has been an accident black spot for several years now, with customers receiving life-threatening injuries on a daily basis as they browse the small shelved area for a range of heavily discounted, short-dated products, including Petits Filous, mince and Zugos microwaveable paninis.

Roberta Clemmins, 36, was admitted to Beaumont Hospital suffering from severe injuries following a rush on

the 'Reduced To Clear' section of a Tesco Express in Fairview, and was pronounced dead shortly after. The daughter-of-two had been lurking by the section while members of Tesco staff stacked the shelves with products nearing their sell-by date. According to eyewitnesses, Ms Clemmins failed to check her blind spots when she made her move and was wiped out by a stampede of old women and students.

Garda Bill Dunne of the Tesco 'Reduced To Clear' Section Safety

Authority addressed the press outside the Tesco Express where mourners have begun to pay their respects using the self-help checkout. 'This morning's incident pushes the death toll at "Reduced To Clear" sections to 17, the highest in four years,' he said. 'We would appeal to shoppers to consider their safety and the safety of others when approaching "Reduced To Clear" sections, and to ask themselves whether or not their lives are worth a prawn salad for 74c.'

Local woman takes grave as quick

A County Laois woman has hilariously beaten her husband to the punch this week after being laid to rest in a plot he had bought for himself in 1996, before they were even married.

Janet Ganley, who died of a massive stroke on Sunday evening, had the final laugh this morning as she was being lowered into the graveyard of their local church.

'She was always stealing my chair in the sitting room,' explained husband Sean Ganley after the service. 'I was forever asking her if she'd take my grave as quick. Then this happens.

Well, I nearly died with laughter myself when I found her in a heap on the kitchen floor. Not a peep out of her, the feckin' chancer!'

Mrs Ganley was pronounced dead by a local paramedic, Steven Taylor, who arrived on the scene some time later.

'It was gas out. The husband was in tears laughing at the whole thing,' recalled Taylor, who admitted that the situation seemed a little weird at first. 'Then he told me about how she was always robbing his seat, and about the whole robbing his grave jibe. It must have taken us an hour to strap her into the gurney with the laughing. Best call-out I've been on in a long time.'

When Mr Ganley bought the plot nearly twenty years ago, he bought it for himself, as he wasn't in a relationship at the time.

'The fact she actually robbed my grave as quick has got me over the whole thing,' he concluded. 'But that was classic Janet – always beating me to it, the gas bitch!'

TRENDING NEWS

New poll shows people prefer murderers to thieves

The latest political opinion polls saw a dramatic increase in support for Sinn Féin, coinciding with a huge drop for both Fianna Fáil and the coalition government of Fine Gael and Labour, proving that Irish people have more faith in murderers than they do in thieves.

Sinn Féin – who were regarded as the political wing of the Provisional IRA throughout the Troubles, but who are now all about gay rights, fixing potholes and whatever else it is they have to do in order to get into government – surged three

points in the poll, conducted by Red C research.

This was in stark contrast to the fortunes of the other main parties, who appear to be suffering the effects of years of lying through their teeth to the public while shafting them for as much money as possible.

'Seems the Irish people are more prepared to forgive decades of death and destruction than they are decades of being pickpocketed,' said Aidan Harper, chief statistical analyst at the Irish Society for

the Obvious. 'So the alleged role of Sinn Féin in the murder of on-duty members of An Garda Siochána, the disappearance of dozens of people who have never been found, punishment beatings, kneecappings ... these things are easier for the Irish people to forgive than politicians handing over billions of euros of taxpayers' money to shady overseas institutions while awarding themselves huge bonuses and pensions.'

Support for independent candidates is said to have held steady since the last survey, indicating that most people are ambivalent when it comes to attention-seekers.

Three dead in Dublin after Cadbury's Creme Egg protest turns violent

Gardaí in Dublin have appealed for calm this afternoon after 3 people were killed and another 17 injured in violent clashes outside the Cadbury's chocolate factory in Coolock.

An estimated sixteen thousand people took to the Malahide Road to protest against the company's new Creme Egg recipe, which they claim is 'inferior' to the original. Beginning online this morning, the protest spilled out onto the streets after the hashtag #DairyMilkOrDie went viral across Twitter in Ireland.

Reports began to emerge last night that the taste of the Creme Egg was different, forcing frantic journalists to contact the chocolatier to find out if anything had changed. Cadbury's confirmed that they had removed the Dairy Milk chocolate in favour of 'standard cocoa-mix chocolate'.

'Cadbury's Creme Eggs are a national treasure,' said one concerned man, who then went into detail about how he 'eats his'. 'I normally bite off the top, before scooping out the creamy middle with my tongue. Then, making sure to coat the inside of my mouth with the creme, I lash into the Dairy Milk chocolate shell. But now that right has been taken away from me.'

Starting in the city centre, the large crowd of protesters made their way to the factory in Coolock, causing massive traffic disruption, and forcing Gardaí to become involved.

'Everything was fine until we got to the factory. Then it all kicked off when some spokesperson for Kraft addressed the crowd, saying, "It's no longer Dairy Milk. It's similar, but not exactly Dairy Milk",' recalled one eyewitness. 'Next thing, someone threw a shoe. Then another person threw a box of Creme Eggs. Then, before you knew it, there were people being thrown at the factory gates.'

Emergency services arrived on the scene shortly after 1 p.m., just before a Garda special response team was deployed. Two men and one woman were pronounced dead, having become impaled on the high fencing around the perimeter of the factory. 'We believe they volunteered themselves to be thrown as missiles,' said one Garda. 'I haven't seen anything like this before, but Cadbury would really want to rethink their recipe.'

Since the incident all roads leading to the site have been closed off by Gardaí, pending forensic examination.

'The arse fell out of the market a few years ago and this explains why,' said city-centre Centra shop owner Gerrard Gormley.

Despite the recent recruitment of new officers and the promise of two hundred more joining soon, many shop owners fear the death knell for their businesses off the back of the recent decline in Garda numbers. In 2008, 1.4 billion breakfast rolls were sold to Gardaí, compared to just 200,000 this year.

'There would be a time where you would have the Gardaí come in and they'd demand the shop be cleared. Then they'd cordon it off with crime scene tape and order, Jesus, about five rolls each,' added Gormley.

In recent times the fall in Garda numbers has resulted in Gormley and many other shop owners taking desperate measures. 'I'd start me working day off standing outside a Garda station with a lovely and hot breakfast roll. The fumes would

Decline in Garda numbers hits sales of breakfast rolls nationwide

Department of Justice figures released today reveal that Garda numbers have dropped in the majority of Dublin city stations, serving as a fatal blow to breakfast-roll sellers nationwide.

waft into them in the station and one or two of them would follow me right to the shop,' explained Gormley. 'But I have a business to run so I can't be doing that every day.'

Gormley also acknowledged the increase in slimline Gardaí – who seem hell-bent on maintaining a

healthy lifestyle – as a real problem too. 'I see now why some people give the Gardaí a hard time. The pricks were coming in here, fitting through the door easily enough, and they'd ask for salads. Do you know how much I spent on widening the entrance to get the fat ones in?' Gormley concluded emotionally.

MEDIA NEWS

Irish media to run a few more Graham Dwyer stories for old times' sake

Despite the tragic story of Elaine O'Hara reaching its conclusion with the life sentence handed down to Graham Dwyer, the Irish media have confirmed that they will continue to run stories on the case which shocked the nation, just for old times' sake.

Architect Dwyer went on trial for the murder of O'Hara, whose body was found on Killakee Mountain in 2013, and was found guilty and sentenced in March. Journalists across the country were initially delighted at being finally able

to call Dwyer all the names they had thought up during the trial, although this jubilation evaporated when they realised they had nothing for the front pages any more.

Dwyer's conviction resulted in a drop in newspaper sales across the board, which media organisations plan to combat by running regular reports on his term in prison, as well as frequent pull-out specials on the entire grim affair.

'Yeah, Graham sure did move a lot of newspapers for us, so we're gonna stay in touch with his story

while he's in jail, just for old times' sake,' said Colm McDonagh, spokesperson for the Irish League of Journalists.

'We're going to do the full Joe O'Reilly on this one: any time we're stuck, we'll just wheel out a Graham Dwyer story. "Graham Dwyer under close watch in jail", "Graham Dwyer receives dental treatment following cavity", "Inside the mind of Graham Dwyer" – pretty much anything at all, really.'

McDonagh went on to clarify that, as the families of those directly affected by the murder case represented such a small percentage of the newspaper-buying public, their feelings about the continuing coverage would not be considered.

In a new awareness campaign launched in Dublin city this afternoon, the Garda Commissioner has warned members of the public to avoid 'broad daylight' if they are worried about being mugged or attacked.

Nóirín O'Sullivan was speaking outside Garda headquarters in the Phoenix Park today. 'Our research indicates that the majority of attacks happen in broad daylight. We would advise people who may be vulnerable to avoid walking on their own in broad daylight if they don't want to be attacked in it.'

A recent study carried out by An Garda Síochána found that attacks in

Gardaí urge people to avoid 'broad daylight' in mugging clampdown

broad daylight were 12 times more serious than those carried out at night-time, and were 43 times more likely to be sensationally reported in the media.

Ms O'Sullivan said that the awareness campaign 'Stay Indoors' will be rolled out next week, and

suggested that those in fear should walk the streets during twilight hours to avoid being mugged, robbed or beaten to a pulp. 'Well, you never hear of anyone being attacked in narrow daylight now do you?' concluded the commissioner. 'It's just basic common sense really.'

BREAKING NEWS

Uncle Ben shot dead by US police

Los Angeles Police fatally injured businessman Uncle Ben this morning after a routine traffic stop went wrong, prompting dozens of people to protest at the site of the killing.

According to reports from the US, the 98-year-old billionaire was driving an orange 2012 Lamborghini Diablo erratically before he was stopped by a highway patrol unit. It is believed the rice tycoon exited the car almost immediately, spooking the police officers and leaving them no option but to shoot him forty-seven times in the head and torso, killing him dead.

'I thought I saw something black in the driver's hand and assumed it was a gun,' explained police officer Kevin Toddson, who admitted to firing the first twenty-three rounds. 'It wasn't until we inspected his lifeless body that we realised it was just his hand on the end of his arm, and not a weapon. Then my partner Gerry told me it looked like Uncle Ben – the rice guy. I fucking love that rice.'

LAPD Chief Mike Burn told reporters that Uncle Ben, real name Gordon L. Harwell, died instantly at the scene before the entire street was cordoned off pending a forensic examination.

Uncle Ben is survived by his son James and three daughters, Tia, Chantey and Maria, who later requested his body be transferred using a large boil-in-the-bag rice body bag, stating: 'it is what he would have wanted.'

The shooting comes at a time of heightened scrutiny of police violence against ethnic minorities across the country.

Sources confirm nation's seagulls have begun uranium enrichment programme

The Irish army has been put on its highest level of alert following reports that the nation's seagull population has progressed from stealing unattended food to working on a uranium enrichment programme in an attempt to build a nuclear bomb.

'We've ignored the warning signs for years – there's no sugar coating the situation now,' a worried-looking spokesman for the army told WWN. 'We all had a good chuckle when they took over Teddy's in Dun Laoghaire and ran the business for the summer, handing out ice cream. But they've obviously taken those profits and got in contact with some dodgy types in Syria – and this is the result: a large-scale nuclear-weapon-building programme.'

Since the turn of the century, seagull attacks have increased by 78 per cent, and have resulted in some 134 unsolved murders. A reluctant seagull, part of their crime empire, is believed to have contacted authorities once he learned of the uranium purchase, believing it was a step too far.

'Their diet in recent years – the scraps of abandoned sandwiches, crisp packets, ice creams and so on – have helped them evolve at an alarming rate, to become more like humans,' explained lead seagullologist Dr Eithne Durkan. 'And just like humans, once they had a bit of cash together, their first thought was to take over the world by building a nuclear weapon.'

Two men arrested as $2.5m shipment of Cadbury's chocolate seized off the US coast

The United States Customs and Border Protection (CBP) agency says field operations officers seized almost three tonnes of pure uncut Cadbury's Dairy Milk chocolate in a small container that was concealed on a yacht that had departed from Ireland.

CBP said officers conducting an inspection of the vessel estimated the street value of the contraband was US$2,498,800, and suspect that it was destined for the underground retail markets on the east coast of the United States.

Two Irish nationals aged 28 and 33 were arrested by armed police who

boarded a vessel called *The Fruit and Nut* at 3 a.m. GMT.

'After a tip off from a rival chocolatier, we stopped and searched the small yacht as it approached a New York City harbour,' explained police team commander Todd Chamberson. 'We found a large shipment of what we believe to be pure Dairy Milk chocolate nine-bars concealed in the ship's hull. Following some oral testing, we confirmed our find and arrested the individuals for questioning.'

It is believed that both men were part of a black-market chocolate ring

based here in Ireland. If convicted of trafficking, they could spend the rest of their lives in a US prison.

Cadbury's Dairy Milk chocolate was banned last week in America, and this is the first known illegal shipment to be stopped by US customs officers.

'This is just the tip of the iceberg,' said New York mayor Bill de Blasio. 'These individuals will be brought to justice. We will treat them as an example to deter others wishing to traffic illegal Dairy Milk chocolate into the United States.'

One of Dublin's biggest toerags has voiced his exasperation at his ever-expanding schedule, stating that he no longer feels that he can commit himself to as much threatening anti-social behaviour as before.

Maurice Gleeson, of no fixed age, made the statement earlier today, saying that years of almost single-handedly lowering the tone of his neighbourhood have taken their toll on him, especially after the deaths or incarcerations of so many of his co-scumbags.

Gleeson went on to state that if he feels he can no longer keep up the hectic pace of full-time scumbaggery, he will begin to favour some aspects of his craft over others.

'I'd rather be really good at a few things than only sorta good at

Scumbag struggles to fit attacks on passers-by into jam-packed schedule

everything,' said Gleeson, steeling himself for another day of doing fuck all.

'First to go will probably be making snide remarks at passers-by in the hope of causing a row with

them. It's a pity because I always loved nothing more than slashing a stranger's face for no good reason. But activities like that keep you away from other things, like robbing old people, or lighting small fires while drinking cans in wooded areas.

'It's just too much hassle, with the Guards and all that. Last time I smashed a bottle over this tourist's head, I was in court for nearly an hour – that's time I could have spent asking people on the bus what the fuck they were looking at.'

Gleeson went on to admit that he would miss the sense of purpose he got from committing random assaults, and didn't rule out giving an occasional dig or two to a member of a minority group, or to a woman walking home on her own at night.

Gardaí celebrate finally making it on to *World's Most Dangerous Police Chases* TV Show

Gardaí involved in the high-speed pursuit of a stolen SUV on Dublin's M50 motorway this morning are celebrating the news that their efforts will be showcased on the American TV show, *World's Most Dangerous Police Chases*.

The perilous pursuit, which saw brave Gardaí risk serious injury in an attempt to stop a criminal who was driving at high speeds, represented a serious threat to public safety before coming to an end in a Jobstown estate in west Dublin.

'We'll be cracking open the champagne tonight, that's for sure,' said Garda John Byrne, who was behind the wheel of the lead vehicle.

News of the ongoing pursuit spread like wildfire via the Gardaí's internal communications systems, which goes some way to explaining why so many Garda cars became involved in the chase.

'As soon as I heard the words "high speed" and "stolen SUV" I knew this was my chance – this case was always going to make it

on to *World's Most Dangerous Police Chases*,' rookie Garda Adam Barry told WWN. 'Sure the Garda Commissioner was in the car in front of me, bursting along. She had the iPhone out and everything, capturing it, ya know, in case the in-car camera was on the blink. No one wanted any screw-ups to stop this from getting on the TV.'

Producers of the hit show were immediately in touch with the Gardaí, sparking joyous scenes at HQ. 'There was a lot of high-fiving and putting on shades afterwards – it was great. It just goes to show: with the right class of criminal, we can really band together to create something worthy of greatness,' Garda spokesperson Elaine Duffy told WWN.

EVERYONE DEAD BY 5 P.M.

THE DARK SIDE OF POTATOES

HEALTH & SCIENCE

DINOSAURS STILL NOT CLONED

NEW REALLY SCARY FLU SOON

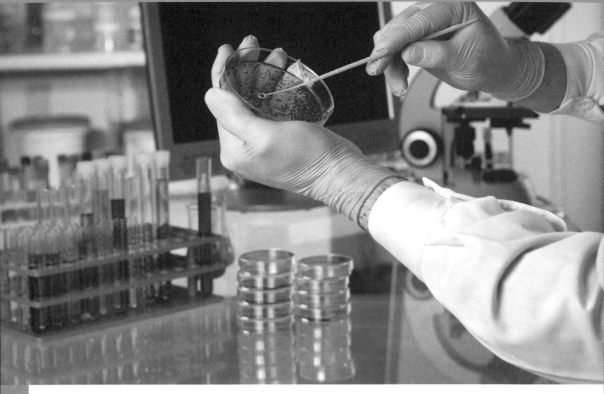

Confidence in scientists at an all-time low as yet another year passes without dinosaur cloning

Public confidence in scientists is at an all-time low as the world's leading scientists continually fail to make the beginning of 1993 blockbuster *Jurassic Park* a reality. A survey conducted on behalf of WWN reveals that, despite various scientific fields advancing the human race in astonishing ways, many people are still using dinosaur cloning as the stick by which to measure their satisfaction with scientists.

Ninety-one per cent of survey participants admitted to feeling continually let down by scientists who, year after year, fail to create clones of dinosaurs that could then be held captive in a thrilling yet poorly secured amusement park.

'I'm not going to lie: I don't know how they get the YouTube videos that small and then on to my phone, but I'm thankful. However, I can't forgive the lack of T. Rex in my life,' declared survey participant and idiot Simon Gormley. 'I thank them again for emojis and that, but how

hard can it be to solve this dinosaur cloning business?'

In the survey, 97.5 per cent of participants listed dinosaur cloning as the key area that scientists should focus on, with reversing climate change coming in a distant second.

'We've done so much good science stuff, but I just feel that if they can't crack this dinosaur thing, what else are they, like, not able to do?' queried survey participant Henry Nolan, seemingly unaware of the little science he himself had done thus far in life.

This drop in confidence could – of course – be reversed if the scientists dedicated more time to dinosaur-

cloning efforts. 'Of course they should be trying. How fucking cool would it be to ride a raptor into work?' asked Shona McGinley. 'Or, oh my God, oh my God, what about those little ones that run around together? How cool would it be if they were your pets?'

Geneticists around the world have admitted that while it would be 'pretty fucking cool' to clone dinosaurs for the public's amusement, it is still not entirely possible.

One hundred per cent of survey participants agreed that geneticists are probably paid too much money and should be forced to work harder in order to make dinosaurs a reality.

Potato addiction: the dark side of National Potato Day

Today marks National Potato Day and while the country rightly celebrates this hardy and versatile food, many media outlets choose to ignore the darker side of potatoes in Ireland.

PR firms have successfully restored the humble potato's reputation since the dark days of the Famine, but not enough is being done to combat the silent killer that is potato addiction.

'I suppose I grew up thinking it was normal, like. Me da did it, me ma did it and now I suppose I've passed it on to my kids too,' shared recovering potato addict Eoin Brophy.

Eoin first discovered his addiction when eating a Sunday roast with his then wife, Aine. 'I lost my temper and just couldn't understand why she was saying I had a problem,' Eoin recalls, reliving the exact moment he was told that having roast and mashed potatoes alongside chips in the one meal was not normal.

Ninety-six per cent of Irish people have found themselves unwittingly addicted to the starch-heavy staple – known on the streets as 'spuds' – sending them spiralling into a well of suffering and bitterness.

'I'm nearly out of the darkness now but, at the height of my addiction, I was spending upwards of €10 a week on a couple of kilos for myself,' added an emotional Eoin.

While a brave few have campaigned for almost thirty years to limit potato advertising to post-watershed slots, they only succeeded in 2014.

'I just got sick of being at a friend's house, or a restaurant, and everyone pushing spuds on me. "Ah, have a chip", "go on, have a roast potato", "only eejits eat salad" – that kind of thing,' said anti-spud campaigner Paddy Murphy.

Yesterday, the influential potato industry agreed to set up and fund SpudAware.ie, a potato awareness resource. Their first ad will be launched next month.

'I've seen an early cut of it and it's powerful stuff,' reported Murphy. 'Just lads talking about passing an awful lot of wind after trips to the chipper; and there was one lad whose dad had been killed by a potato to the head. Sad stuff.'

National Potato Day will be followed by Potato Addiction Awareness Month this November.

BREAKING NEWS

Irish blood transfusion service seeks urgent donations from everyone except queers

A steep drop in blood donations has prompted the Irish Blood Transfusion Service (IBTS) to issue an urgent appeal for the public to come forward and donate blood, just as long as they aren't some sort of homo.

With the stock of blood units at an all time low, people are being urged to visit their nearest donation clinic to give blood, with the proviso that they mustn't be a man who has had

another man's penis enter his body at any stage in his life.

'I'm just doing my bit to help out,' said Sean Conlon, who – despite riding strange women at every given opportunity – is allowed to donate as much blood as he can. 'You know you're helping out somebody who badly needs it, and you never know when you might need a transfusion yourself. Plus, it only takes a half an hour, so I

can get back to whoring around as much as I like before too long.'

In an official statement issued this week, the IBTS was quick to state that, while they point-blank refuse blood from men who have had sex with other men, even if a condom was used at the time, they aren't discriminating against homosexuals in the slightest.

'Gay men are more than welcome to donate blood,' said William Eaton, chief spokesperson for the IBTS, 'just as long as they've never had any form of sex with another man. If you're a gay celibate virgin, then by all means land in and we'll take your blood. But if you've had so much as the tip of a penis inside your mouth or bum at any stage of your life, then we ask that you keep your filthy blood to yourself.'

Gym guy hospitalised after tiny T-shirt cuts off circulation

A Dublin-based fitness fanatic has praised the members of the emergency services who rushed to his aid on O'Connell Street yesterday after he collapsed with a suspected case of blood loss to the brain caused by wearing a T-shirt that was several sizes too small for him.

Cathal Hennessy, originally from the Midlands but now living in Dublin while he studies at UCD, is an avid bodybuilder who trains several times a week to achieve his impressively bulked-up physique.

On top of a gruelling workout regime and strict protein-heavy diet, Hennessy also wears T-shirts and jumpers bought in the kids' section of Penneys in an attempt to emphasise his huge arms, toned abs and the absence of a discernible neck.

Despite it not being that warm yesterday, Hennessy was wearing a Transformers T-shirt suitable for kids aged 9–12 when he began to feel faint while walking up and down O'Connell Street looking at himself in shop windows.

Described by onlookers as being incredibly pale in the face while having arms that were going purple, the Athlone native collapsed outside Easons, where he was treated by the staff of a passing ambulance.

'Mr Hennessy was incredibly lucky we were in the vicinity – if we'd had to travel, he might not be here today,' said paramedic Martin Ashford, who was first on the scene. We were able to discern that his collapse was caused by his T-shirt being so tight that it was cutting off his circulation. We cut the garment off, allowing the blood to return to his head, reviving him almost instantly.'

Hennessy is the fifth gym freak to be involved in such an incident so far this year, with many health officials concerned that the number will only rise during the summer. Gyms across the country have been urged to place tight-T-shirt warnings in their facilities, to warn muscle fanatics of the dangers involved in borrowing their little brother's clothes.

Mothers that breastfeed attend hero awards ceremony at Dublin Castle

Irish mothers, and the long-ignored and vital part they play in Irish society, will finally get the recognition they deserve this evening at the Hero Awards at Dublin Castle.

Specifically, mothers who breastfeed their children will receive medals from President Michael D. Higgins, but those mothers trying to gain access to the ceremony who have not breastfed their children will be shot by snipers from the roof of Dublin Castle.

Talking about breastfeeding, which is a perfectly natural thing that no one over the age of two is really that interested in, had been controversially banned under Irish law and was punishable by death. However, in recent years, the draconian attitudes to a mother feeding her child have had an amazing turnaround.

'God, there was a time, I remember, when I was talking to another mother about breastfeeding and before I knew it, I was arrested by the Guards. It's nice to know now we can be acknowledged in a small way,' said breastfeeding mother-of-two Lorna O'Sullivan.

Experts have confirmed that mothers who breastfeed should probably stop being so shy about pointing out that they do in fact breastfeed.

'A lot of mothers are very modest – they don't like to make a fuss about it, so it's only those mothers who post four thousand status updates relating to breastfeeding who will be rewarded at tonight's ceremony,' confirmed one of the event's organisers Terry Reilly.

The ceremony at Dublin Castle is expected to last for three hours and organisers have promised that a fireworks display costing €300,000 will take place once the ceremony is finished. The inspirational song 'True Colours' by Cyndi Lauper will play on repeat throughout the event.

Narcissist makes his cancer diagnosis all about himself

A 24-year-old narcissist has made his recent cancer diagnosis all about himself, much to the displeasure of his friends and family.

Sales rep Colm Healy hasn't shut up about his testicular cancer diagnosis since he found out about it earlier this morning, prompting many people who know the egotistical narcissist to speak out.

'All right mate, you're not the only one with shit going on in their lives, yeah. Pipe down,' wrote Colm's best friend Alan Dunne in response to an email Colm sent friends and family informing them of his diagnosis.

'It's just take, take, take with him,' Colm's mother Deirdre explained to WWN, adding that she was sick of listening to Colm talk about how his diagnosis will affect him. Colm, for his part, just won't shut up about it.

'I'm actually quite scared, to be honest. I'm not sure where to turn,' Colm said, seemingly unaware of how self-centred he sounded to everyone else.

'Not one mention of what happens to his PlayStation 4 if he kicks the bucket. It's all "me, me, me" – it makes you sick,' Colm's younger brother Jack told WWN, taking issue particularly with the fact that his brother has not clarified what would be added to Jack's collection of expensive products in the event of Colm's death.

'If I could get a word in edgeways, maybe I'd find out, but it's narcissism ville, population Colm right now,' Jack concluded.

Average human attention span shorter than this headline

The latest study of the average attention span of humans reveals that it is so fleeting that the entire content of this article is redundant.

Researchers at the International Institute of Studies have discovered that the attention span of the average human is so short that you have most likely already been distracted from this article by something shiny or the bright screen of your phone.

'I mean I'm happy to tell you how we arrived at our conclusions, but because of those very same conclusions, I know also that the vast majority of the human race is so blindingly stupid that they've already gone chasing after a cat that's popped up by the window in their sitting room, or just decided to put this article down in favour of practising fart noises with their armpit and hand,' explained the lead researcher Dr Gregory G. Jones.

'Honestly, I'm almost sure that you've become distracted while interviewing me. In fact, I just saw you check your watch there. Christ, now you're taking a selfie despite my efforts to tell you about all this. Well, at least we know our research is conclusive. Hello? Seriously, I'm right in front of you – stop sctraching your crotch,' he added.

The benefits of making this research public are as yet unknown, as it will prove incredibly hard to get people to concentrate on the meat and bones of the information.

Local 'character' actually in need of some serious help

Local character Mossie Daly, beloved of locals in the Dungarvan area is – on closer inspection – actually in need of some serious fucking help.

Always good for a laugh and a chat outside the majority of pubs, off-licences and Centras in the area, Daly has for years ambled back and forth across roads, encountering, obliging and smiling at local residents.

However, it has now been suggested that his happy and playful manner is not purely down to the fact he is a 'character' but due instead to crippling alcoholism that everyone has at some point witnessed but chosen to ignore.

'I had him help paint the clubhouse there last year, ya know, to give him a bit of money. You wouldn't get more craic out of an individual, always has a story,' explained local GAA enthusiast Gar Hill, going on to reference the time Daly sang 'Sweet Caroline' from the roof of the clubhouse at 1 a.m. while completely naked.

'Aha, some character,' confirmed Hill, openly discounting the fact that Daly is behind on his electricity and heating bills after spending the money he borrowed from his sister on drink.

A number of locals have confirmed that the place would be duller without him, and that you wouldn't get that sort of craic outside of Ireland.

Daly is believed to thankful for the regard in which he is held as it will come in handy next weekend when he drunkenly smashes the window of Tesco only to be let off the hook by the local guard.

New cigarette packaging to feature pictures of your dad riding your mam

A new incentive to stop young people from smoking will see branded cigarette packaging replaced with sexually explicit pictures, potentially featuring their very own parents.

The news comes following a survey which suggests that recent campaigns to curb smoking among young people – which have included plain, unbranded cigarette packaging as well as packaging adorned with graphic images of the negative effects of tobacco – are having little to no effect.

It is hoped that this latest scheme, which involves the help of tens of thousands of parents across the country, will be a major breakthrough in the war against tobacco, and enough to put kids off cigarettes for life.

'Plain packaging has no effect, health warnings have no effect, so let's see how kids cope with paying a tenner to see a picture of their parents going at it like dogs on heat,' said Sean Ashcroft, chairperson for the Irish Anti-Smoking League. 'The photos are donated by the parents and will be randomly placed on every cigarette pack in the country – so no matter where you are or what brand you smoke, you run the risk of buying a pack and seeing a full-colour image of your dad lashing your mam out of it.'

Trial versions of the packs have been rolled out across the country. So far only one Mayo teenager has been unlucky enough to have purchased a pack of Benson & Hedges featuring a picture of his mother getting driven into the ground by his dad. After he stopped crying, the young boy confirmed that the experience has put him off cigarettes for life.

Toothpaste scientist not sure how much more advanced product can get

World-renowned toothpaste scientist Professor Conrad Lee admitted today that his team is all out of ideas when it comes to further advancing the product, claiming they have already created every possible formula.

Lee, who works with several toothpaste manufacturers across the world, believes the industry should 'quit while it's ahead' and not continue to reinvent something that just basically cleans your teeth.

'I'm probably shooting myself in the foot here, but I think we've taken this toothpaste thing as far as it can go,' said the 46-year-old. 'Seriously, you can't reinvent the wheel over and over. Last week we advanced an advancing advancement – I'm getting dizzy just thinking about it.'

Since 1896, Colgate has already sold over five thousand versions of the same thing. Lee claims that producing multiple versions of the same product can be counterproductive as it suggests the original wasn't that good to begin with.

The scientist also slammed the animated adverts that depict the product as some high-tech cleaning agent developed in sophisticated laboratories.

'This whole thing is just getting ridiculous,' he added. 'It's basically soap for your teeth.'

To date, leading toothpaste brands have made wild claims regarding their products, which include advanced whitening, sensitive formulas and even glitter toothpaste for those seeking sparkling teeth.

'I'm done with the whole thing,' Lee concluded. 'I'll probably look for a job in the washing powder industry or go into nappy development or something.'

Really scary animal-flu news story due soon

Hundreds of Irish people may die and thousands more will suffer serious bouts of anxiety from watching intimidating animal-flu news bulletins, an expert group of Waterford scientists has warned today.

It recommends that citizens should consider avoiding all forms of aggressive news propaganda during such periods and just carry on with their everyday lives. It also says that Ireland must stockpile an anti-bullshit attitude in the event that there is another media outbreak.

The experts who drafted the report say that it is almost inevitable that another animal-flu pandemic will be blown out of proportion but it is impossible to predict when.

Dr Colm Williamson, a leading expert on bullshit, stated the average time between each of the last four pandemics was about five years.

'We're due another one very soon,' he said. 'Its name will probably include some kind of living creature. If I was to put my money on it, I would guess that it will be fish flu. We've already had bird flu and swine flu. I think a creature from the sea would be a good bet this time.'

He also claimed that the current economic climate is causing an anti-government mindset, and that this alone is good reason for a new media flu outbreak.

'I don't think the governments of the world have much choice. A good old-fashioned flu scare should quench any burning ambitions of revolution. It will have to be a good one this time. None of this "just-old-people-and-young-babies" crap. This one will have to put the willies up everyone to work properly,' he added.

The report also says that, in the event of another government-sponsored media pandemic, television news stations should be declared infectious diseases under existing laws, requiring all viewers to block them with the aid of their parental controls. These can be found by pressing the menu button on the television remote control.

Currently, 24-hour news stations are not a specified infectious disease.

Thousands of Irish people killed with the heat

A national day of mourning has been announced by the government following the highest number of people killed with the heat in recent memory.

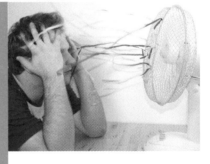

Ireland's heat-related death toll has reached four thousand since the beginning of the summer, with the middle-aged and elderly being the worst hit.

No county in Ireland has escaped the crisis – even holidaying couples have sent poignant messages home from abroad reporting that they too were killed with the heat.

'It's nice here, but I'm pure killed with the heat,' wrote Jennifer

Keenan in a Facebook message to her sister earlier today. The 31-year-old, currently on holidays in Lanzarote, hasn't been heard from since.

'Our sincerest condolences go out to the families of those that have been killed with the heat,' said Jack Meighan, spokesperson for Met Éireann's 'Crisis Containment' division. 'We would urge anyone who fears they're about to be killed with the heat to stay as cool as

possible, maybe put the window of the car down a bit, or sit in the shade until the threat passes. If someone beside you says they're killed with the heat, make every effort to cool them down as quickly as possible. Push them into the nearest body of water you can find.'

There are fears that this year's tally of people killed with the heat will become the country's highest weather-related death toll since the gory aftermath of January 2013, when ten thousand people were skinned with the cold.

Dock leaves no longer available without prescription

There was more bad news today for people who frequently fall down in large clumps of nettles, after it was revealed that dock leaves would only be available with a prescription from September onwards.

The decision was met with fury from parents and children alike, who know that the in and out motion of a dock leaf, combined with the singing of a rhyme describing the motion, is the only thing that will take out the sting of a nettle.

Although currently freely available over the counter, obtaining dock leaves will require a trip to a GP from September, and must be administered in a pharmacy by a trained dermatologist who will sing the rhyme to the patient and dispose of the dock leaf in a special Hazmat bin.

'This is ridiculous. I used to be able to fetch my ball or whatever from a clump of nettles, sort it out with a dock leaf and be back playing in minutes,' said Kevin Devlin (9).

'Now I have to go to a GP, sit there for ages, go to the chemists and get dock leaves that way. Plus the dock leaves they have in the chemist are these weak, generic dock leaves, not the good ones that you used to be able to get. It's all a money racket!'

The move has been met with the same negative backlash as last year's ruling which saw parents no longer allowed to hit the ground and tell it that it was bold after their kids fell on it.

Dublin lad dislocates shoulder throwing shapes

St Vincent's A&E department was last night faced with yet another troubling case of a Dublin male being admitted with a dislocated shoulder due to excessive shape-throwing.

Throwing shapes has been an important part of Dublin culture for the last century, as hard-as-nails bastards and hard-as-nails bastards-in-training seek to stamp their authority on the air around them by pulling aggressive moves on the city's streets.

However, as part of the evolution of throwing shapes, young inner-city males have become increasingly extreme in their movements, with experts warning that severe injuries are a real risk.

One victim of the craze was 14-year-old Smithfield resident Anto Daly, a self-described 'mad cunt'. While spending the day with friends, indulging in some harmless intimidation of the elderly, Daly looped his shoulder too fast and too wide, resulting in a popping noise, later revealed to be a dislocated shoulder.

'We're now the premier specialists in this country at putting hard-as-nails bastards' shoulders back into place,' explained Dr Peter Curran of St Vincent's. 'Despite our best efforts, we find the same people coming back into A&E as they just can't seem to curb themselves. We just urge everyone out there to throw their shapes responsibly.'

In the most alarming case ever recorded, 29-year-old Deco Kinsella lost both his arms in 2009 after repeatedly ignoring warnings about excessive shape-throwing.

Waterford student suffocates inside her own make-up on girls' night out

A County Waterford woman who collapsed and was subsequently pronounced dead at a city centre nightclub last night has been named as 21-year-old Janet Keane, Gardaí have confirmed today.

The woman, who was studying French and Business at Waterford Institute of Technology, is believed to have suffocated inside her own make-up shortly after leaving the women's toilet at 11.30 p.m.

'Jan said she was going to put on some more make-up before we hit the dance floor,' recalled the victim's friend, Dorothy Hazelburn. 'One of the girls pointed out that she was struggling to keep her head up due to the weight of it all. I asked her to take it easy on the foundation as her whole face was slipping – her eye-holes were down around her cheeks and she couldn't even see where she was going, the poor pet.'

Unfortunately the granddaughter-of-four failed to heed the warning and continued applying even more make-up.

'She looked a right mess when she came out of the jacks,' explained another friend, who was too upset to give a name. 'Her HD brows were more VHS at that stage. When I looked closer they were just under her nose like a moustache. She insisted on going dancing – despite the Groucho Marx head on her!'

Security at the club confirmed that Ms Keane got about halfway to the dance floor before collapsing 'like a bag of spuds'. 'I thought she was drunk so we threw her out the exit doors,' admitted head doorman Barry 'Basher' Hollihan. 'It was nearly "Uptown Funk" time again so we didn't want to see her get trampled on either.'

The bouncer later defended his decision, citing the club owners' strict 'no tolerance rule on intoxication', despite the venue being a well-known student bar that promotes €3 drinks.

It is believed the victim's friends followed her outside and called an ambulance. Janet Keane was pronounced dead at the scene and an early morning post-mortem found the young student had suffocated to death inside her own make-up.

Since the story broke, local TDs have jumped at the chance to call for better education on make-up application for the under 25s.

EXCLUSIVE

Black-and-white Facebook profile picture indicates you are 'going through some stuff', study shows

A new study conducted on behalf of Facebook has revealed that the vast majority of people who choose to have a black-and-white photo as their Facebook profile picture are 'going through some stuff'.

'In all honesty, is there a better way to communicate such an existential quagmire? I don't think there is,' said Leon Mulaney, sociologist and lead researcher on the Facebook-commissioned study.

The study – which involved surveying a sample of ten thousand people who had recently switched to a black-and-white photo – revealed that 91 per cent of those who did followed up the change in the next few hours with a 'going through some stuff'-related status.

'There are several degrees of deeply held feelings, and often an individual is so sorrowful that their feelings can manifest themselves not only in a black-and-white photo, but also one in which the person is staring off into the distance rather than looking at the camera,' Mulaney added.

Admittedly, some of the black-and-white profile pictures contain happy, smiling individuals, but Mulaney insists he is certain their motivations are just as melancholic.

'A picture of a smiling, happy person in black and white? It's just their way of saying, "Look at me, so happy, so content. This will be gone when I'm dead, any chance of a comment or a like?" If anything, that type of profile pic conveys even higher levels of going through some stuff.'

Facebook has said it will take the information from the study on board and is already planning to prevent teenagers who have only just discovered Nirvana – some of the biggest black-and-white photo abusers – from using non-colour profile pictures.

Doctors baffled after Dublin girl turns scarlet

Dermatological experts at one of Dublin's leading hospitals are said to be 'baffled' by a case in which a teenage girl appears to have turned completely red.

The 17-year-old, who cannot be named for legal reasons, was admitted to the Mater Misericordiae University Hospital yesterday lunchtime, accompanied by several of her worried friends.

Reports suggest that the teenager was travelling to the city centre on the bus when she exclaimed, 'I'm scarlet!' It is believed that her friends, who had been playing Tiesto songs loudly on their phones and

yelling for no good reason, initially failed to grasp the severity of the situation.

'She was always saying she was scarlet about this and that, so we just ignored her when she started up this time,' said one of the girl's 16-year-old friends, who does not wish to be named because it's none of your bleeding business.

'But then we looked at her and, true enough, she had litch turned red.

Maybe from claiming to be scarlet all the time? We don't know. In case it's contagious, I'll just say I'm embarrassed for her, and also for her mother for having her in the first place.'

Doctors who examined the teen in A&E have yet to issue a statement clarifying what exactly turned the teenager scarlet, but they are confident that she will return to her normal orange shade before too long.

Entire nation to freeze to death by 5 p.m.

Characteristically unprepared for weather that other nations would sunbathe in, Ireland faces a complete freeze by about 5 p.m. today, with the entire population certain to die.

A variety of reasons for total annihilation has been provided by Met Éireann in its extensive report entitled *Snow: Ah, What the Fuck Do We Do?*

Met Éireann had recommended that the public should wear an additional seventh layer of clothing, but it is thought that this measure, along with watching *The Day After Tomorrow* for tips, will prove futile. It is estimated that the last Irish person alive will die by 5 p.m. while trying to clear snow from their footpath.

'Snow transforms a person's very being. Their psychological state is often altered and they become a danger to society,' confirmed leading psychologist Daniel Adams. 'Much of the Irish public is elated at the first sight of snow but loses all reason and logic once the conditions begin interfering with everyday tasks like driving. A normally docile man will be driven to murder if his trousers become covered in that awful slush snow can turn into.'

The low temperatures currently being experienced in Ireland are such that the tempers of rational people are becoming uncontrollable. 'Snowball attacks have increased by 65 per cent in the last twenty-four hours,' confirmed Sergeant Vincent Mackey.

Gardaí admit that their resources are stretched to breaking point after much of south Dublin was lost in a huge avalanche earlier this morning.

'In the blink of an eye almost all of them were gone,' explained Sergeant Mackey. 'The avalanche was caused by the cries of passion of a retired couple who engaged in a particularly vigorous bout of lovemaking while on a morning walk up the Dublin mountains. The snow started rumbling along after climax.'

Government as we know it has collapsed since the Cabinet took the government jet to the Bahamas to escape the cold temperatures.

EDIA WELCOMES LATEST TRAGEDY

POPE SMACKING LESSONS

INTERNATIONAL NEWS

MUHAMMAD DRAWING CONTEST

JUDAS HOMOSEXUAL MANUSCRIPT

America celebrates its national holiday

Under sunny blue skies that hinted at spring, thousands of Americans lined both sides of Manhattan's Fifth Avenue this afternoon, waving flags to mark the country's national holiday, April Fool's Day.

Led by former US president George W. Bush, the colourful ticker-tape parade made its way slowly through the New York streets to the cheers of spectators hoping to get a glimpse of passing floats commissioned by various corporations and organisations in the city.

2015 marks the 334th year since the death of the USA's patron saint, Saint April Fools. 'As you can see, there is a huge turnout for this year's event,' Mayor of New York Bill de Blasio told WWN. 'I think Saint April Fools would be proud if she was alive today. It's great to see such a huge number of people enjoying the spring sunshine.'

Saint April Fools, who died in 1681, was anointed patron saint of America in 1862. Sister Fools, originally from Spain, travelled to the free world in 1664 to help convert native Americans to Catholicism, and soon became famous for her generosity and meat sandwiches, which she later christened 'hamburgers'.

'She invented the burger as we know it today,' explained historian David Humphries. 'Saint April Fools was a good woman who helped the sick and fed the poor. Native Indians called her "Kaka Koo Choo", which translates as "pear hips" in English. She was also a bit of a joker and liked to play pranks on patients by hiding their money and goods for long periods of time.'

It is understood that the popular saint died of coronary disease – believed to be caused by her high-protein, low-vitamin diet – at the ripe old age of 38. Some two hundred years later, American president Abraham Lincoln sent a letter to Pope Pius IX, asking him to anoint April patron saint of America. The Pope granted his request later the same year.

BREAKING NEWS

Media welcomes latest tragedy

After a rather slow news week across the board, the world's media gathered as one this afternoon to welcome the latest news tragedy to fill our papers and screens. Editors and sub-editors raced to allocate potential story ideas to thousands of hungry journalists, who had all but lost faith in the unpredictability of the world and its peculiar workings.

'I was sure the week was going to drag,' said one *Daily Mail* journalist, who was writing a piece on Kanye West's shoulder tattoo at the time, 'but I think we'll get a good month out of this one. Plenty of families involved. Lots of glorious misery to play around with, too. Great for business.'

As fragmented details filtered down the news assembly line, many journalists were ordered to simply 'copy and paste' from major news sites for the moment – until potential angles were discussed by the hierarchy responsible for making the shocking details into workable headlines that will attract readers.

It is only thirty minutes since the awful event, and online publications are already awash with articles reworked from previous tragedies that were similar in nature in a bid to hold readers. Informative and in-no-way tasteless Top 10 lists of previous tragedies helpfully inform readers that previous tragedies of a similar nature have also taken place in the past.

Additional work has also been created for journalists who will write a missive criticising the lustful exuberance of the media in its efforts to gain any semblance of a 'breaking news' piece.

Many publications will successfully convince their readers that they take no pleasure in commodifying human suffering despite the opposite being true.

'The views on this are going to be amazeballs,' offered *The Sun*'s editor David Dinsmore. 'This couldn't have come at a better time in the week to be honest. A large and rather gruesome court case is wrapping up so at least now we have something to fill in the gaps. Hopefully there will be some foul play involved or speculation; and if there isn't, we'll hint at some anyway.'

Terror experts are said to be disturbed by the behaviour of callous and barbaric ISIS forces after discovering they are doing everything in their power to keep out of the headlines.

'This is probably the most devilish conduct I have ever seen from a terror group in all my time covering them,' veteran Middle East reporter David O'Callaghan told WWN.

Sources in the region confirmed that ISIS has abandoned plans to launch a number of cats from cannons into a nearby wall for their own amusement after learning of the devastating pressure exerted on an American dentist following his slaying of an innocent lion.

The negative publicity has seen ISIS carefully select their future targets in a bid to avoid widespread

ISIS staying out of the headlines by not killing lions

online pressure and abuse from the public.

'They've certainly adapted and changed tack. They've shelved all animal cruelty plans and chosen to focus on things that don't horrify and anger the public as much, like the beheading of an 82-year-old academic,' terror expert Simon Perceval explained to WWN. 'This really is the most terrifying and sobering move in their campaign of terror: that they

have chosen to behead, maim, kill and rape humans knowing full well that there will be no large-scale opposition movements online.'

Citing the fact that the average person received over four thousand requests to sign a petition to protest against the killing of a lion, experts believe that ISIS could continue to avoid being splashed across the front page of newspapers and websites if they continue with their calculated decision to leave animals alone.

Pope to show Catholics how to smack their children properly

In yet another reminder of how ridiculous the notion of receiving instructions from an elderly celibate who talks to a man in the sky is, the Pope is now to show Catholics how to beat their children properly.

Pope Francis has gained popularity since becoming pontiff thanks largely to selfies and people ignoring all the horrible subjugation he still stands behind —but now the Argentinian faces sharp criticism from parents.

Priests are now famously known for not being allowed to be alone in a room with a child, but this hasn't stopped the Pope from trying to provide parents with a guide on how to smack while leaving the child with their 'dignity' intact.

Utilising his zero years experience of child rearing, the Pope is to produce a 'how to' DVD based on a number of workshops he conducts in the Vatican.

'Yes, I have found it very helpful,' explained parent Julio Gomes. 'Before the workshop I used to try and reason with my child, but now that Il Papa has told me that smacking your child is totally on trend right now, as a good Catholic, who am I to refuse?'

The DVD based on the Pope's smacking workshop – *It's What Jesus Would Have Wanted* – is expected to hit the shops in the coming weeks, with early reviews suggesting that the Pope gives a smacking showcase.

'With guidance on everything from the small "polite tap" to the "not the face, everyone will see the bruises",

we the audience are left in no doubt as to who can lay the smackdown to end all smackdowns,' wrote *Guardian* film reviewer Tuppence Smith. 'Viewers will find it hard to forget catchy mantras such as "if your hand don't sting, it ain't no thing".'

However, not everyone was impressed with the Pope's latest venture.

'He can fuck right off,' explained parent and general ignorer of religious leaders Victoria Flynn.

The news of the Pope's new DVD release has come at the same as his launch of a conference on the protection of minors.

'See, this is why the Vatican is a crumbling wreck of archaic ideology and hasn't a fucking notion,' explained religious affairs journalist Conor Jeffries.

It's What Jesus Would Have Wanted retails at €9.99 and is available from all good shops.

German marches against stereotyped minority probably nothing to worry about

The world has confirmed that a large-scale protest in Germany against an easily stereotyped minority is probably nothing to worry about, and that no comparisons to any other period in Germany's history should be made.

'Let's just see how this shakes out, for Christ's sake. Don't get angry about a bit of peaceful protest,' pleaded historian Alison Dickinson.

Some 18,000 people turned out in Dresden in a protest against Islam that was organised by a group calling itself Patriotic Europeans Against The Islamisation of the Occident (PEGIDA).

Despite Muslims making up just 6 per cent of Germany's population, PEGIDA's neo-Nazi leanings have seen its marches take on a decidedly xenophobic tone, with support for the group growing slowly.

'Ah, this should be just fine – I can think of literally no other period in European history that had similarly inauspicious beginnings. It'll be fine, honestly,' explained Professor of Contemporary European History at Berlin University, Wilhelm Beckermann.

Islam, known to many as a religion which encourages people to gorge on freshly born babies, is supposedly prone to being misrepresented in the media, but there is still little evidence of this occurring.

'Look, I think it would be a good idea to leave PEGIDA to it, and come back in a few years and see if, you know, there's something to worry about,' Deiter Kruger, a leading opposition politician in Germany, told WWN.

A poll carried out by *Stern*, a German weekly news magazine, saw 30 per cent say they believed Islam had so significant an influence in German society that PEGIDA marches were justified.

'History is there to be studied the night before an exam in order to scrape an easy B; it's not there to be learned from,' said political commentator Simon Gruber.

The same *Stern* poll indicated that one in eight Germans would join an anti-Muslim march if it took place in their locality.

Religious experts contributing to internet forums often use acts of terror carried out by people claiming to represent Islam as a way to criticise the entire religion, in much the same way as they don't claim all Catholics are evil for the part they did not play in priests abusing children.

Angela Merkel has confirmed that she will attend an upcoming PEGIDA protest and stare and tut disapprovingly in an effort to bring an end to these xenophobic marches.

EXCLUSIVE

North Korean internet outage due to leader using land line

An ongoing internet outage in North Korea today was played down and described as nothing more than 'a busy line', with officials stating that the glorious leader Kim Jong-un was responsible because he'd picked up the landline to make a call.

Since this morning, the entire state has been without access to the world wide web, spurring fears that the country was under cyber attack from the United States.

The loss of service came just days after President Obama pledged that the US would launch a 'proportional response' to the alleged attacks on Sony Pictures, which government officials have linked to the hermit kingdom.

'Our glorious leader decided to call Russian president Vladimir Putin to wish him a happy Christmas and a prosperous new year,' local state media reported. 'This call was long and full of promise. We have now secured new allies against the filthy mutt dogs in the West.'

Addressing worried viewers, the announcer asked everyone to ignore such outages in the future, as they were just the great leader using the phone, and to be patient while he gets up to some serious business with his new-found friends.

The entire country's internet is currently sourced to a 54k modem in the presidential palace. Officials claim that 'proper broadband' is currently being installed and should be operating in the new year, relieving pressure on the phone line, and preventing any further embarrassment.

God considering turning humankind off, then turning it back on again

Following a long and arduous attempt to get humanity to act the way he initially intended, God admitted that he was considering just unplugging us, leaving us for thirty seconds and then plugging us back in.

The statement comes as the world deals with yet another week of violence and hatred, which was punctuated by the senseless slaughter of 142 people, mostly children, in a Taliban attack on a school in Pakistan.

Having attempted several hardware upgrades as well as keeping the world updated as often as he can, God has finally admitted that there may not be any option other than to switch humanity off and then turn it back on again, hopefully restoring the world to its factory settings.

'Humanity isn't supposed to be this way, but everything just keeps crashing,' said God, who doesn't think that a worldwide society which lives in harmony for all eternity is too much to ask for. 'I've banged on the world a couple of times to see would that set things straight, but every time I log in, all I see is people killing each other, usually in my name. I installed a few updates which I hoped would sort things out and I even sent the young lad down once to have a look, but that only seems to have made things worse.'

Clearly exhausted, God went on to admit that many of the atrocities committed by humans may be a result of poor decisions made when setting up the system in the first place. 'Okay, I'll admit I installed a few "free-will" add-ons for humans that showed up in pop-up ads at the start,' said God, who has been on hold with customer support for ages. 'I thought they'd be good, but they just seem to have corrupted the whole thing. I also opted for the free versions of human behaviour programmes rather than paying $10 for the premium versions. I thought I was going to save money, but all that has happened is people killing each other in droves for the most pointless of reasons.'

Should God decide to switch humankind off then switch it back on again, it will be his second such action. God initiated the first – the great flood which washed away the entire population of the world except Noah, the Ark and everyone inside – by pushing a pin into a small hole at the back of the world.

6 Reasons why Jesus is voting Yes in the Marriage Referendum

As almost everyone knows by now, Jesus Christ sensationally broke his 2,000 plus years of silence to tell the public why He is voting Yes in the upcoming marriage equality referendum. WWN has gathered some of His reasons below in a handy list.

1) Despite His reservations, Jesus admitted that the referendum is only about the question of equality and 'I had a pretty good track record on that'. Although he understands Catholics who say 'traditionally, marriage is between a man and a woman and has been for thousands of years', the Saviour pointed out that nailing people to a cross had also been a tradition at one point as well as not giving women the vote, and treating black people like second-class citizens.

2) Freddie Mercury is Jesus Christ's favourite singer of all time and He often accompanies the singer on piano in Heaven, with 'Don't Stop Me Now' being a particular favourite.

3) On His blog 'Just Jesus Things' the only Son of God said that the fact that the Law Society of Ireland has explained clearly that a Yes vote will not legally alter the rights of the child has swayed Him to the Yes side. He also cites the fact that the Special Rapporteur for Children has reiterated that the 'same-sex marriage referendum won't change adoption in Ireland' as well as the endorsement of a Yes vote by leading children's charities. He added that 'someone who blindly ignores the testimony of experts when it comes to children probably isn't thinking of the children at all and is merely trying to prop up their own conceited dogma'.

4) Jesus's barber in heaven is a gay Filipino man named Greg, who has been dyeing our Saviour's roots for years and who 'seems like a nice, harmless guy'.

5) Jesus also disclosed that he was surprised that the No side representative in an RTÉ debate on *Claire Byrne Live*, Senator Ronan Mullen, had been so vociferous about the importance of the rights of children, considering he is the former spokesman for the former Archbishop of Dublin Desmond Connell, who was heavily criticised in the Murphy report into clerical abuse for failing to report his knowledge of child sexual abuse to the Gardaí.

6) Jesus chose not to broach the emotional subject of His two dads, instead opting to explain that some of His best friends are No voters but that doesn't mean He has to jump to conclusions without first knowing the facts like they often do.

Americans not sure if they need more guns – or fewer

A massive shoot-out between rival biker gangs in the Texas town of Waco, which left nine people dead and hundreds more in police custody, has once again prompted Americans to question whether they need to get rid of guns or buy loads more.

The killings, which officials believe may have been related to some biker feud, came during a mass brawl between three gangs of grown men who clearly don't know any better. Starting with knives, chains and clubs, the warring factions eventually remembered they were Americans and began to shoot each other as fast as possible.

Gardaí, known in America as the police, soon arrived on the scene and began exercising their rights as set out in the Second Amendment to the Constitution. When the dust settled, dozens of bikers were dead, dying or injured, and Americans were once again caught in a debate over whether they should change gun laws or go out and buy as many pieces as they could.

'To gun or not to gun?' mused Arlene Harrison, a Waco resident who was in the vicinity of the bar where the deadly brawl broke out. 'On one hand, I'd like it if I could walk around my town without worrying about people with guns everywhere. On the other hand, when shit goes down, a gun would be a fairly useful thing to have. I don't have a gun at the minute, but after seeing all those biker guys shooting at each other, it does seem like it would be mighty handy.'

As citizens across America continue to scratch their heads, politicians and senators are adopting the same 'wait and see' stance on gun control that has served them so well over the past 239 years.

Daily Mail changes name to *Daily ISIS*

British tabloid the *Daily Mail* and its online sister the *Daily Mail Online* have announced their names will change from next week.

The newspaper's editor Paul Dacre explained the changes at a London press conference this morning. 'The *Daily Mail* will change its name to the *Daily ISIS* as part of our rebrand, which we will be launching in April,' said the 66-year-old. 'My decision to reinvent the newspaper follows feedback from our readers who want nothing more than to read ISIS-related material involving beheadings, immolations and executions, and how the events are somehow the fault of a Middle Eastern-looking shopkeeper from Hull.'

Mr Dacre – who is also the editor-in-chief of dmg media, which publishes the *Daily Mail*, the *Mail on Sunday* and the free daily tabloid *Metro* – explained that online news readers are becoming ever more voyeuristic and that people's thirst for blood and violence has become the key editorial motivation for the publication. He promised that more pixelated videos and graphically descriptive content would be made available for its ghoul-starved readers.

'We're just going to give the people what they want,' he said. 'Most of our online traffic these days comes from articles describing despicable human acts of torture and depraved sexual conduct. People love it! This move was a no-brainer.'

The paper also announced it will publish a daily 100-page pull-out called 'The Abuser', which will contain some of the world's most horrific sexual abuse cases, covering everything from child abuse to bestiality.

'Our top viewed stories are child abuse articles,' he confirmed. 'It's what people like to read. It's there in the web page analytics so don't pretend to get all shocked about the fact. We're here to sell papers and not lessons in conscience.'

Keeping with tradition, the *Daily ISIS Online* promises still to add shocking titles above the articles that it posts on Facebook in a bid to intrigue readers. 'Expect words like "disgusting", "horrific", "outrageous" and "gruesome" to appear as usual,' concluded the editor. 'We actually employ people for the sole purpose of coming up with these titles, so it would be a shame to put them out of their jobs.'

Police in Garland, Texas, shot dead two would-be attackers yards from an event which dangled a $10,000 prize for the best drawing.

'A fucking brilliant idea,' local police chief Howard Schumann said after putting his and his officers' lives on the line so that the American Freedom Defence Initiative (AFDI) could host an event which had the clear aim of offending a particular religious group.

'Yeah, from the outset we had a really good feeling this event would go off without a hitch,' said Schumann sarcastically, 'and I've since learned that ISIS are claiming responsibility for the attack so "yay shitty art competitions".'

The overtly anti-Muslim organisation AFDI had set up the cartoon contest in a bid to utilise America's much vaunted freedom of speech protections. It is understood that the freedom of speech event did not accept any irreverent cartoons of Jesus because that would be truly offensive.

'I treasure my freedom of speech deeply and I'm willing to use this

Muhammad cartoon-drawing contest goes about as well as expected

Experts in common sense have confirmed that a Prophet Muhammad cartoon-drawing contest organised by right-wing conservatives in America went about as well as expected.

freedom in a provocative manner, safe in the knowledge that ultimately it will be some solider or policeman who will be killed protecting my rights, not me. And that is why America is the greatest country in the world,' explained the event's chief organiser Pamela Gellar.

Freedom of speech on non-religious grounds appears to be very important to right-wing conservative groups in Texas: just two years ago the state Senate passed a law which stipulated that secular schools could be decorated in wall-to-wall Christian holiday decorations in the month of December. It is presumed there was no provision in the Senate

bill for the religious observance of Ramadan.

Gellar previously made headlines this time last year when she erected anti-Muslim advertisements, calling for all foreign aid to 'Islamic countries' to be cancelled. She also believes that 'secret halal meat' is being sneaked into school lunches in America.

'We're all about equal rights for all,' Gellar explained, 'but it's just that some of our rights are more equal than those of Muslims.'

Experts offering their opinions on these latest events have agreed that all religions in the wrong hands are equally offensive and damaging.

Man who eats 'the Body of Christ' at Mass can't believe the latest Scientology documentary

Dublin man and father-of-five Donal Lyons scoffed and nearly spat out his dinner while watching eye-opening Scientology documentary *Going Clear*. Sitting down to watch TV with his youngest son Cathal, inquisitive father Donal couldn't quite believe how mental some of the followers of 'this so-called religion' are.

'Ah, Cathal, what is this shite you have me watching? *Aliens*?' Donal asked, expressing his astonishment at the frankly idiotic people

portrayed in the film who found themselves drawn into this the disturbing cult.

Cathal began pointing out to his father that he attends church every Sunday and, in taking communion, believes he is eating the flesh of the 2,000-year-old son of a space alien.

'Ah, now Cathal, don't get cheeky. Just look at these lads in the film. Singing and dancing about how "they're on the right path". They'd be

committed to the insane asylum over here,' Donal explained carefully.

One particularly shocking part of the *Going Clear* documentary focused on how a pregnant woman was forced to live in jail-like conditions while being made to carry out manual labour.

'See, Cathal lad, you can't make comparisons to our religion. Just look what these nut jobs are doing. That poor woman,' said Donal.

However, Cathal and Donal found common ground when the documentary focused on Hollywood actor John Travolta, with both men agreeing that he was a bit creepy, even if they couldn't put their finger on exactly why that was.

WWN Guide to
Smacking
your child
and getting away with it

The European Committee of Social Rights has found that Ireland violated a European charter by not banning all corporal punishment, including parents smacking their children at home, so here at WWN we have put together a couple of lifehacks for smacking your child, or smack-hacks as everyone in the office here likes to call them.

It's not smacking if the wooden spoon is doing it

Convince your child that the wooden spoon is actually a magical instrument. Explain to them that they are made from the same wood as magic wands, but instead of magical powers, they deliver magical beatings to children who are bold. We would suggest distancing yourself from the spoon's actions by shouting at it to stop when hitting your child. Pretend it has a mind of its own and that you are not in control of its clearly violent nature. Acting upset with the spoon's lashings will convince your child that you are not the one to blame here for the pain being inflicted. It's the spoon. Spoons can't get arrested.

Hire a neighbour or a friend to administer punishment

Again, distancing yourself from smacking is essential to avoiding arrest. Soliciting a disguised neighbour or a friend is a great way of doing this. You can also take turns hitting each other's child too, and this can become a bit of a fun game once

you get into the swing of it. If your child is acting up just leave the room. Say nothing at all. Leaving the front door open, ask your sponsored smacker to call around and deliver the beatdown while you pretend to go to the toilet. Your kid won't have a clue who it is and when it's all over you can just explain that it must have been one of Santa's helpers checking up on their behaviour. Tell them if a Santa's helper calls more than five times in a year they get nothing for Christmas. This is our favourite one on the list.

The old midnight soap in a sock technique or 'blanket party'

Featured in the film *Full Metal Jacket*, this clever little smack-hack allows you to personally hit your child without leaving any visible bruises. Best done at night while your kid is asleep, and ensure you have your spouse, partner or friend with you to hold down your child. After checking that they are fast asleep, get your accomplice to throw a sheet over your child making sure to cover their whole body so they can't see or move. Then, with your soap in a sock, beat them around the torso area, making sure not to connect with the ribcage. We advise 30–60 seconds of this, depending on what they did. Once administered, leg it out of the room and into your own bed. Watch as your bold child hobbles into you for sympathy. Don't give them any and blame it on a bad dream. Tell them bad dreams happen when you're bad.

Make them hit themselves

Threats of selling them to the tinkers not working? Well, why not try this age-old smack-hack which inadvertently forces your child to hit themselves.

This is best performed in a playful manner by pinning your toddler to the ground with your knees while grabbing both their hands and forcing them to hit themselves in the face. Say stuff like 'why are you hitting yourself?'and 'stop hitting yourself' and so on. Be playful but firm. Beware, though, as this will only work with younger children who don't know any better. The best people at this are the ones who convince the child to actually hit themselves when bold. Hard to do, but worth it in the long run. Once mastered, the child soon becomes self-harming, letting you sit back without the worry. Bad child. Bad.

special *feature*

Lost Vatican manuscript reveals Judas was gay

New evidence released this week claims that Judas Iscariot, one of the twelve original disciples of Jesus Christ, was a 'raging homosexual' who tried to force himself on the Son of God numerous times.

According to a two-thousand-year-old manuscript unearthed in the Vatican vaults, Judas regularly made advances towards his fellow disciples, and was quoted as saying he would 'kiss Jesus on the lips at some point, whether he likes it or not', no matter what the consequences.

'It appears that Judas had a thing for our Lord Jesus Christ for quite some time,' confirmed Federico Lombardi, director of the Holy See Press Office, 'so much so that he ended up betraying Jesus to the Romans after Jesus turned down his sexual advances. This explains why the Catholic religion frowns upon such practices today.'

Lombardi stated that there have been several explanations in the past as to why Judas betrayed Jesus, but that this latest find details his four-year-long crush on Jesus in stunning detail.

'Judas was always the first to volunteer to wash the Lord's feet,' he said. 'There are also references made by the traitor to Jesus's physique, claiming that the Lord's abdominal muscles were quite ripped for a man of his age, and that he used to dream about rubbing ointment on them after supper. Following several years of harassment, Jesus eventually told Judas that he wasn't into that kind of thing and urged him to stop watching him bathe as it was getting a bit creepy.'

'Being a gay,' continued Lombardi, 'Judas didn't take rejection well and ended up betraying Jesus by kissing him in the garden of Gethsemane – embarrassing him in front of his disciples and a band of Roman soldiers.'

According to the newly discovered manuscript, the first ever homosexual mentioned in the bible was so struck down with emotion after betraying his love that he took his own life before descending into hell.

'Jesus died for the sins of all mankind,' concluded the Vatican spokesman. 'Womankind? Not so much.'

ISIS MOVES TO IRELAND

DO GAY PEOPLE EAT CHILDREN?

LOCAL NEWS

LOCAL LAD TRIES TO BE ARTY

FARMVILLE POTATO FAMINE

Twelve injured as bridesmaid lunges desperately for bouquet

Ambulances were called to a wedding reception in the Carlow area this weekend following one woman's single-minded bid to catch the wedding bouquet.

It is widely believed that the person who catches the bouquet will be the next to marry, and this traditional view is thought to have influenced the perpetrator's aggressive lunge for the flowers.

Bridget Nally, a 37-year-old Carlow native, is reported to have leapt maniacally toward bride Emma Nolan's bouquet as it soared 12 feet above the dance floor at the Mount Wolseley Hotel.

'It all seemed jovial enough, but then there was this kind of guttural yell,' explained one of the injured wedding guests, Laura Campbell. 'Then I felt a foot in my back and I realised that I had unwittingly become Bridget's stepladder to the bouquet.'

Several single women were jockeying for prime position around the dancefloor while Bridget's boyfriend of nine years, Paul Higgins, attempted to distract her with the promise of shots – but to no avail.

'We were on the scene almost immediately. It was one of the most gruesome sights I've ever seen,' a paramedic told WWN. 'There was a pile of contorted bodies on the ground – some with broken limbs due to the ferocious impact caused by the individual who was hell-bent on securing the bouquet for herself.'

Bridget remains unapologetic, proclaiming 'Get fucking in! Time to go dress shopping, bitches.'

It is expected that Bridget will marry Paul within the next five years, after she has slowly ground him down.

Wexford native Cathal O'Downey has admitted, on condition of anonymity, that he is quietly delighted that his eldest daughter, 19-year-old Grainne, hasn't blossomed into an attractive woman.

'She's all gangly limbs and, God love her, she's got my chin, and nose, and teeth, and ears, and – Christ – that forehead,' Cathal told WWN after a few pints in his local. 'I'd steeled myself in anticipation of, you know, young people antics, fellas with the horn trying it on with her. But if you were to catch a glimpse you'd understand why I'm just made up that she's no oil painting.

'You couldn't sell her if you tried, and I'm delighted. I can sleep at night knowing she's not doing the unmentionable with some lads' lad,' Cathal added.

Father secretly delighted that daughter has blossomed into unattractive woman

Cathal explained that his intense love for his daughter has meant that he only wants the best for her and that has led to him wishing she remain a virgin pretty much her whole life, unsoiled by the grubby hands of undeserving 'gobshites'.

'You know it was touch and go there for a while when she turned seventeen. You can ask the wife – we were almost certain everything was coming together to form a knockout but it just didn't come together. No debs date or anything. She's been up in Dublin at college for a year now and nothing; not a sniff of any lad going near her,' Cathal explained.

'Some of my mates have been telling me about the knowing looks you get from the young fellas who are after having their way with the daughters, but I've yet to see it, thank God.'

Nation feeling tricked as gay men start marrying their dads by the thousand

Irish citizens who voted Yes in the recent marriage equality referendum are today feeling pretty stupid as recent events – such as gay people marrying their family members for tax purposes – have proved that the No voters were right all along.

The referendum about same-sex marriage in Ireland took place on 22 May, with 62 per cent voting in favour of the amendment. That 62 per cent of the electorate are now feeling the bitter sting of 'I told you so' from those who voted against.

Since the passing of the bill, thousands of gay men have been united in matrimony with their fathers, brothers and uncles – just as predicted by campaigners for the No side.

With nothing to stop the LGBT community from marrying whoever they want, 100 per cent of gay people have rushed to take advantage of the tax credits and benefits allowed to married couples.

'I just feel so cheated,' said Maura McMahon, who voted Yes after failing to heed the warnings of campaigners on the No side. 'I thought the church and the Iona lads and that Dublin footballer were all talking shite, but here we are at the end of days: surrogacy rates have skyrocketed, designer babies are being made-to-order, straight lads are marrying themselves for the craic ... We were wrong, we were so, so wrong.'

WWN was unable to obtain a comment from the LGBT Society of Ireland: its members claimed to be 'too busy pulling apart the fabric of society' to make any statements.

ART NEWS

Local lad trying way too fucking hard to be arty

A Dublin man is trying way too fucking hard to be arty, claiming he's suddenly interested in strange pieces that appear quirky and abstract and that no one else gets.

Terry Mackey, who has spent the last six years of his life being

unemployed, changed his online work status to 'artist', much to the surprise of family and friends who know him 'too well'.

'Dole artist more like,' pointed out sister Mary Mackey, who admitted being sick of his pretentious bullshit lately. 'Terry bought a stripy scarf and one of those blazers last month and thinks he's Andy fucking Warhol all of a sudden. All he does is hop from one exhibition to the next, availing of the free wine. It must be great to have no job and to just talk shite all night while sleeping all day.'

Mr Mackey, who crushed fourteen empty cans of Bulmers with his forehead last Paddy's Day, denied that his recent interest in art is just a phase, stating he used to 'always love drawing on desks in school.'

'I think the education system in Ireland held me back if I'm honest,' he told WWN, also blaming peer pressure from classmates for picking metalwork instead of art for the Leaving Cert. 'I'm like a blossoming flower that has been left in the shade for most of its life. Now that the sun is shining on my weary petals, I can only get brighter and more colourful.'

In a series of rather odd pictures of himself staring deeply into a mirror, the stay-at-home son of two announced that he will be organising his own exhibition very soon and would love if everyone could make it along.

'I'm gonna call it "reflections of the self",' he explained on the Facebook events page he created, before inviting all 1,435 of his friends. 'You don't have to understand my art to appreciate it. Just soak it in. It is what it is.'

A County Longford man has vowed to keep his lips sealed in future when passing people he doesn't know on the street, after being blanked for the umpteenth time this week.

Charlie Price, who moved to Dublin last year, admits he hasn't been able to kick the habit of greeting passers-by since leaving his home town, pointing out that Dublin people are nowhere near as friendly as the folks back home.

'How hard is it to say hello back?' asked the 28-year-old, not getting a reply from this reporter.

'Seriously though, people up here don't even acknowledge each other. I've been sharing an apartment for the last year and have had literally

zero conversations with the two guys I live with.

'What's that all about?' he asked again, now obviously realising he wasn't getting an answer.

Price went on to describe a rather strange and peculiar phenomenon in Longford where, he claims, everyone says hello to everyone else, even if they don't know who they are.

'Am I talking to myself here?' he then asked. 'Will this be in the paper like?'

Leaving the culchie where he stood, this reporter could not help but notice his overly clingy behaviour, and pondered whether this may be where his problem lies – that in fact his own insecurities

Culchie living in Dublin still finds himself saying hello to passing strangers

drive this uncontrollable urge to reach out to his fellow human beings, regardless of whether he knows them or not.

Jimbo Halligan, 16, acquired the 125cc shortly after his birthday, but claims to have bought the bike himself despite not having any income.

'His mother bought it for him 'cause the father ran away with some young wan,' said classmate Gerry Roche, who spotted Halligan chatting to some girls in the Lidl car park earlier. 'All he does is drive around the town thinking he's great. No one likes him at all. The girls only talk to him cause he's got a bike. I heard he shit his pants in Junior Infants.'

While no one is entirely sure as to the origin of the motorbike, every pupil around the town is in agreement that Halligan, who has managed to get a string of girlfriends thanks to his bike, is a complete prick.

Carefully driving down Main Street, the grandson of four revved his engine ever-so-slightly while passing a bunch of hooded teenagers, before accelerating off at speed, but still adhering to the strict 50km per hour speed limit.

Young fella in Fifth Year has motorbike

Some young fella in Fifth Year has a motorbike and likes to sporadically pull up beside loitering school friends for no apparent reason, it has been revealed today.

'He does that every fuckin' time, boys,' shouted sixth-year student Tommy Daly angrily, as he smoked with friends he made through smoking down the back lane after school.

'I heard his mam's an alco and slept with Mr Brent from economics class,' confirmed Daly, who it is believed was promised a hand job from Ciara Lyons at a free gaff last weekend but who missed out when she gave one to Halligan instead once she saw that biker jacket on him.

Halligan has become the subject of near universal derision due to his ownership of a motorbike

that no one else from school would be caught dead on, obviously.

'I hope he gets hopped off the thing,' remarked 16-year-old Jason Ryan, who was expelled from school last year for setting fire to a cat, and who is in no way suffering from intense jealousy. 'If he revs it one more time around me I'll tear him off and kick his teeth in.'

FUTUREWATCH
ISIS MOVES TO IRELAND

In a not-too-distant future, Islamic extremist group ISIS will relocate to the Midlands in a bid to extend its terror network. WWN takes a look at life in this parallel Ireland ...

1) THE GUARDS MORE OR LESS LEAVE THEM TO IT

Every now and then, a headless body shows up, dumped on the side of a road near Mullingar, but no one ever gets arrested. Guards issue statements that the victim was 'known to Gardaí', but that's about it.

2) THE POLITICAL PARTY THAT REPRESENTS ISIS DENIES ANY KNOWLEDGE OF ITS ACTIVITIES

The members of a Muslim party, described by many as the political wing of ISIS, fervently deny any connection between the two groups. The party leader, Jehri Ad-hamns, claims no knowledge of how Panti Bliss came to be flung off the side of the SIPTU building.

3) ISIS VIDEOS BEGIN TO CONTAIN MORE REFERENCES TO 'SHITE IN A BUCKET'

Videos of jihadists executing hostages are now shot on shaky Nokia phones and uploaded to YouTube. Islamic dialect has been replaced with a harsh Midlands twang, and infidels are now referred to as 'dogshites'.

4) DENIS O'BRIEN MAKES A FORTUNE BY GOING INTO THE ARMS BUSINESS

Naturally.

5) BEHEADINGS ON MONDAYS DECREASE AS JIHADISTS RING IN SICK

Executions and terrorist activity plummet after weekends, bank holidays, lads' birthdays etc. The heads of ISIS call a staff meeting stressing that all absences must be explained with a doctor's note, as texts saying you're 'not able' will no longer be accepted.

TRANSPORT NEWS

Luas bell to be replaced with voice yelling 'get the fuck out of the way'

A spokesperson for the National Transport Authority has announced new measures to cut down on the number of collisions between Luas trams and members of the public – the introduction of a new system to warn people to 'get the fuck out of the way'.

The recording will replace the more familiar 'ding-ding-ding' bell currently in use – Luas drivers have repeatedly reported that pedestrians, motorists and cyclists fail to heed the existing warning sound.

The move follows the release of driver-cam footage of motorists and cyclists blatantly disobeying stop signals and racing across the tram tracks, often barely missing the oncoming tram. Facing claims that the bell warning is too dainty or just not threatening enough, the NTA claims it has no choice but to replace it with something that people might pay attention to.

'People hear the bell and pass no remarks about it,' said Ambrose Bermingham, spokesperson for the National Transport Authority. 'So we have no other option than to get more aggressive. The "ding-ding-ding" sound was designed to be a polite way to warn people of oncoming danger, but seeing as how they don't respond to it, we feel a voice yelling "get the fuck out of the way" will better help people to get the fuck out of the way.'

With the system set to be in place by early 2016, Luas staff are currently voting on who they would like as the voice that yells, with Liam Neeson and Twink reported to be front-runners.

Average Leaving Cert student asked about Leaving Cert 3.47 times per second

Research released today has revealed that students sitting the Leaving Cert are asked about it an average of 3.47 times per second, which seems to suggest that the entire nation is ignorant of the huge pressures felt by students sitting the exams.

'Oh, the Leaving Cert! Not long now, eh,' is the phrase most frequently used by friends, family and complete strangers when they address one of the fifty thousand students sitting the exams, with the unintended consequence of driving the students to the brink of lunacy.

'I know some people mean well but, fuckin' hell, it's grating,' explained Carlow student Kevin Burke, who became so frustrated by questions about his upcoming exams that he decided to get 'Yes, I'm doing the Leaving Cert. Not sure what points I'll get. Yeah, I'm doing honours Maths. Commerce in UCD, hopefully' tattooed on his forehead.

Students have banded together to launch the 'I am more than just the Leaving Cert exams I sit' campaign, aimed at encouraging people to converse with them on any subject that isn't related to the Leaving Cert.

'I'm that sick of all the LC talk that I'd happily talk about how much I masturbate at this point – honestly I would,' explained Alan Cummings, a Wexford student.

Some reports in the media have even suggested that there are bands of elderly people roaming around, approaching anyone who looks 'Leaving Cert age', just so they can torture them with questions about the exams.

It is also thought that relatives of students use the exams as a sort of conversational crutch to lean on as they honestly haven't a clue what to say to a 17- or 18-year-old half the time.

'It just seems like a good-to-go topic,' explained Maura Jennings, whose niece is sitting the exams this year. 'I'm just being polite – I couldn't give a shite, really, but I don't want her to know that.'

Worried parents of Leaving Cert students have moved from politely pointing out that the exams are on the horizon to actively trying to convince their children to cheat.

'We've had to get the Gardaí involved several times in the last few days,' a Department of Education spokesman told WWN. 'One parent in the Dublin area had hired a plane with the intention of writing all of his son's notes across the sky as he knew his son would have a clear view through a window in the exam hall.'

Will gay people eat my children?

Gay people, like any other class of people, are prone to bouts of cannibalism and infanticide, so in essence, yes: it is true to say that they want to and will eat your children.

I heard that two men got married in New Zealand just for the laugh, even though they're heterosexuals. Will that happen here?

That's the problem with heterosexuals – if they're not getting gay married in New Zealand for a laugh, they're getting straight married in Las Vegas for a laugh. Unfortunately, heterosexual marriage is legal the world over.

I am still undecided. Is mustering the energy required for me to pick a side really worth it?

Of course not. The opportunity to positively or negatively affect the society you live in is better off left unrealised.

Homicide and 'the Homo Side' sound very similar – should I be worried?

You are 100 per cent right, they do sound similar – well done for spotting that. However, this is mere coincidence. There are no sinister overtones to this one I'm afraid. Although now that I think about it a bit more …

'Will gay people eat my children?' and other referendum questions answered

Prior to the marriage equality referendum in May 2015, WWN reached out to prominent experts to help answer some of the Irish public's most pressing questions about the vote.

I go to Mass. Is my opinion more important than facts?

Sadly it is not. Facts, beloved by the Yes campaign, are made out of graphite and reinforced steel, whereas the opinions of churchgoers are made mostly of soggy grass.

I'm cold.

I'm sorry but that is not a question – it is a statement.

Are homosexuals, famed for their aggressive natures, bullying conservative Catholics and unoppressive tendencies, into voting Yes?

Despite the very real 'homo agresso' stereotype, the homosexual community is merely using readily available, nearby supplies of logic to suppress a small percentage of conservative Catholics.

For fuck's sake, will someone just tell me definitively – is it about 'the children' or not?

It is not about the children. It is about equality ... but then they told us 9/11 wasn't an inside job.

Will 1950s Ireland cry if the referendum passes?

More than likely, yes.

Some of my best friends are gay people who don't deserve the same rights as I do.

Once again, that's not a question, more of a statement. A horrible statement, actually.

Sorry, just making sure here now, but is it about the children?

Ah for fuck's sake.

special feature

Waterford man didn't even read that *Guardian* article he just shared there

Local man Kevin Bridges shared yet another article from the *Guardian* online today in a bid to gain kudos from his learned mates, despite not actually reading the 768-word piece at all.

After spotting the headline on a friend's Facebook page, Bridges quickly realised the article's potential as one of those 'intellectual posts' that would stimulate lengthy debate among those friends who just love to show off their vast array of knowledge.

'It's about American foreign policy in the Middle East or something,' he told WWN, admitting he was not really bothered about its content. 'I'll kick things off with a "classic America" comment to get the lads going, and then just mirror what everyone else is saying. Hopefully no one will challenge me too much on it,' he added.

Refreshing his post some five minutes later, Bridges's *Guardian* article had already gained four likes from the very friends he was aiming to impress.

'Watch now, Gerry from work liked it first and hasn't commented yet. It's gonna be a long juicy one packed with useless facts, I bet,' said the 28-year-old onesie fan. 'Hopefully Niall from school will step in with some stupid conspiracy theory. Always fun to mock.'

Following the successful post, Kevin Bridges confirmed a total of fourteen likes and fifty-six comments, pushing him further up the social media ladder of intellectual fame.

'I even got away with a direct copy and paste from Wiki in one of my comments,' he concluded. 'My work here is done.'

The game, in which players manage the operation of a virtual farm by harvesting crops and raising livestock, has proved incredibly among tablet and smartphone users, but is most popular on Facebook, where players can send requests to their friends to help them with their virtual homestead.

Irish players had taken to the game in their thousands and were enjoying the fruits of their labour until a devastating digital blight fell on the potato crops, crippling virtual farms across the land.

With players now struggling to keep their farms running, many have opted to leave the game and set up a new life elsewhere.

'I've had to leave behind a herd of pretend cows and sheep, as well as over thirty acres of make-believe land,' sobbed Martin Hennessy, the once-proud Farmville player whose entire potato crop was destroyed.

'I spent hours upon hours building that farm from scratch, only to see

Thousands of Irish players leave Farmville following devastating potato famine

Following a crippling drought that swept across the digital farmlands of popular online resource-management game Farmville, vast numbers of Irish players have decided to leave and go elsewhere.

my hard work disappear overnight. Lunch breaks, bus journeys, lying awake at night ... and now it's all gone. There's nothing left for me to do except download a different game and try to build a new virtual life elsewhere.'

The Farmville Famine will go down in history as the worst mobile gaming disaster of our times, easily outdoing the devastating Jelly Invasion experienced by Candy Crush players last year.

TECH NEWS

Fucking idiot old person doesn't know how to use ATM

Some fucking idiot old person doesn't know how to use the ATM and should be in a home, a large queue of people have said today.

Paddy Farrell, (probably about 90 or something), spent over six and a half minutes trying to extract money from a busy city centre

bank machine, apparently totally oblivious to the twelve anxious people behind him.

'He didn't even turn around to say sorry for his stupidity,' said third in the queue Darren Regan. 'I don't know how many times I tutted and made impatient gestures at him. Like, it's lunchtime, old man; let some of us who still have a life left go through.'

Struggling to see the screen in the bright sunlight, Mr Farrell was heard murmuring something about his reading glasses, not that anyone cared.

'People like that should have minders or something,' whispered

Tracey Phelan to another lady, who was already late for her two o'clock hair appointment with Peter Marks. 'Retired people should not be allowed into the city centre during business hours. It's a disgrace.'

After finally hitting all the right buttons on the cash machine, Farrell also managed to hit all the wrong buttons with those behind, by loudly releasing a putrid cloud of gas from his corduroy-curtained anus.

'Hope they choke on it, the impatient bastards,' he told himself, walking away calmly, as if his fart was a cool Hollywood explosion.

Man needs the end of *Trading Places* explained to him a few more times

Carlow man Aidan Martin has announced that he is three, maybe four, viewings away from understand the ending of the popular '80s comedy *Trading Places*, in which protagonists Louise Winthorpe and Billy Ray Valentine use the stock market to get rich while bankrupting the villainous Duke brothers.

Martin, 35, has always enjoyed the Dan Aykroyd/ Eddie Murphy movie, but admits that he's never really been that sure what the fuck is going on once they get to the stock exchange.

'Okay, so everything up to the bell ringing on the exchange floor, I totally get,' said the Carlow native, who never passes up the chance to watch the movie when it's on telly.

'And then ... I dunno. Everyone just starts yelling and shouting, there's numbers everywhere, and then all of a sudden the Dukes are broke while the other two lads are rolling in cash. I get that they knew about the orange crop report, and switched it ... actually, no ... I don't even know what the fuck all that was about.'

The actual explanation for the ending to the fish-out-of-water romp has eluded audiences for decades, with even director John Landis admitting that he 'took the writers' word for it'.

Despite the head-scratching finale, Martin has assured the public that he will continue enjoying the movie at every opportunity, in particular the scene in the jail cell and the bit where Jamie Lee Curtis takes her top off.

2015 Leaving Cert papers to be written entirely in emojis

Following reports of record levels of borderline illiteracy in today's teenagers, the Department of Education has revealed plans to publish this year's Leaving Certificate exam papers in a combination of emojis, emoticons, and text-speak.

The move follows worsening Leaving Cert results, which many experts have attributed to the rise in smartphone communications, in which proper spelling and grammar have been cast aside in favour of smiley faces and acronyms.

Exacerbated by social media platforms such as Snapchat and Twitter, this problem means that today's student now has trouble reading plain English, let alone writing it.

In a bid to combat the falling grades, a spokesperson for the Department of Education today announced plans to publish exam papers written in the same nonsense that kids are used to reading every day. 'The ability of a teenager to form a coherent sentence has nosedived in recent years,' said Owen Caughlin, spokesperson for the Department of Education. 'This has led to a drop in performance across the board when it comes to the Leaving Cert. We were going to issue spelling waivers, similar to those we offer to dyslexic pupils, but in the end, we thought it would be easier just to write the exam papers using a combination of LOL-speak and wee pictures of cats high-fiving each other.'

Following the implementation of the emoji system, the Department of Education will next look at an overhaul of test marking, with the current points system expected to be replaced with Likes and FAVs.

Man reading the *Irish Times* on Luas hopes somebody notices

Obviously intelligent Niall Ahern spent much of his early morning commute to Dublin city centre on the Luas displaying his copy of the *Irish Times* to anyone who cared to presume he was superior to them for reading it.

Mr Ahern, 31, was travelling on the Luas at 7.35 a.m. but didn't let the early hour deter him from catching up on the most important news from here and abroad.

'Could I just download the app on my phone? Yeah, of course, but then who would know I was reading the *Irish Times*? I once gave the app a trial run, but people found me a bit weird for laughing and saying 'oh, classic *Irish Times*' just to let them know that's what I was reading – so I reverted to the cumbersome broadsheet,' Ahern revealed exclusively to WWN.

Despite the lack of space on the Luas, Ahern made sure to secure both a seat and airspace for his copy of the paper, and nodded and smirked as he read. 'It's not enough just to read it – I have to make a song and dance about flicking through the pages. A particularly loud tut is always good,' explained Ahern.

Ahern went on to reveal that when he looks up from the paper, appearing to contemplate the complex ideas put forward in the opinion pages, he is really just checking to see if anyone is staring at him in awe. 'Now, it's around Ranelagh that I sometimes find myself nodding off because the news is boring as fuck in fairness, so I sometimes pinch myself, or if there's no helping it, I take a quick nap behind the paper.'

It didn't take Ahern's fellow passengers long to notice the 31-year-old's intimidating intellect. 'It was a bit annoying at first to be honest – his elbows were jutting out and over on to my seat, I had page five stuffed in my face and started to feel shit about the fact I couldn't pick out Syria on a map, and here was this lad reading about it,' explained irritated commuter Paul MacAuley.

'But I suppose it wasn't all that bad when he got to the page with the cartoons on it and then the sport. I started giving that a read and then went back to watching videos on my phone.'

Before disembarking at Stephen's Green, Ahern almost ruined the illusion of great intelligence by mistakenly flicking to the last few pages of the paper which include the weather and some other shite that no one ever reads.

Wicklow field infested with Dubliners in mobile homes

A field adjacent to Wicklow's beautiful Brittas Bay has become infested with Dubliners thanks to the southward seasonal migration of the urban pest, WWN can reveal.

Enclosed in makeshift nests known as 'mobile homes', the Dubliner has become an increasingly familiar sight in these parts when temperatures rise.

'Look, I'm used to it at this stage,' explained local Tom Crainey. 'I suppose you're just thankful it's not a bank holiday weekend, ya know? If they come anywhere near the driveway, I usually bang some pots and pans – that startles them and they run away.'

The usually empty beach becomes inundated with large groups of Dubliners who often travel in groups of more than four. This urban pest is known to enjoy disrobing and rubbing itself in water and sand before marking its territory using several black sacks full of rubbish.

'They are curious in nature and often head to the surrounding areas to sniff around and explore,' explained leading Dublinologist Padraic O'Brien. 'The male Dubliner is also known to shake the caravan from side to side vigorously as he mates with the female.'

Local Wicklow residents have in recent years begun to withdraw from seaside locations in an effort to limit their exposure to the Dubliner.

'Oh I've heard you can catch almost anything off them, so no, from April to September, I wouldn't be caught dead near the beach,' explained visibly shaken Wicklow resident Catherine Duffy.

REELING IN THE YEARS

ww news
Waterford Whispers News

Taoiseach John A. Costello confirmed today that all children attending school in Ireland would receive a complimentary pack of cigarettes, courtesy of several benevolent cigarette manufacturers.

The health drive, backed by all medical practitioners on the island, will see each child's right to a pack a day enshrined in the constitution.

'We've seen obvious advantages to children picking up the habit at a young age,' confirmed the head of Marlboro in Ireland.

'And might I add that no, there are no adverse health effects, so I'll just stop you there before you even ask,' added general practitioner and supporter of the initiative Michael O'Donovan.

In a presentation delivered to Waterford Whispers News, the government outlined the savings that they stand to make by introducing this novel, ahead-of-its-time scheme.

'Children have tiny lungs, so they won't smoke as much – that's point one,' explained a government spokesman. 'And obviously smoking helps with concentration and nourishes the child, so those less well-off families save on food – there is literally no downside to this.'

The government confirmed that an annual smoking fun day would take place, with prizes for the child who could smoke the most cigarettes in one sitting. The first day of the initiative has already yielded some positive results, with no participants dying. The scheme will be extended nationwide as of tomorrow.

'CIGARETTES IN SCHOOLS' PROGRAMME BACKED BY GOVERNMENT

Wednesday, 24 November 1949

INTER-COUNTY MARRIAGES FINALLY LEGALISED

Wednesday, 6 June 1979

Taoiseach Charles Haughey addressed the nation in a broadcast televised on RTÉ last night to reveal that his government is discussing the possibility of legalising inter-county marriages.

'It is an open secret that the number of these unions, which some would describe as unholy, has increased in recent years. We must act to reflect this change in society which sees Kerry man lie with Cork woman, Dublin girl courted by Galway man,' the Taoiseach said as he opened his address.

There are reports that many hard-line same-county marriage advocates became ill while listening to the address, but it is believed that this will have little bearing on the sea change that has recently occurred in Irish society.

Although banks have granted mortgages to inter-county couples for some time and they have enjoyed many of the same freedoms as same-county couples, a stigma has persisted. With the government legislating for the change in law, it is thought that, over time, this stigma will dissolve.

'We now take the leap that will see us, in years to come, remembered as the generation that said a county border should be no barrier or impediment to love,' the Taoiseach said, bringing a close to his address.

The impending legislation will also see the removal of the troublesome 'man may lie with sheep as he pleases' provision in the constitution which has plagued rural communities for hundreds of years.

POPE GIVES COURTING COUPLES RIGHT TO SHIFT BEFORE MARRIAGE

Monday, 24 March 1983

His excellency Pope John Paul II granted courting couples across the world the right to shift before marriage during a landmark Mass delivered from St Peter's Basilica in Rome yesterday evening.

In a move that is set to change the Catholic dating world forever, the pontiff advised that shifting be allowed under certain circumstances, providing that marriage has been agreed between the two parties.

'Couples must have a verbal contract of matrimony before any shifting takes place,' he explained. 'The man must initiate the shift before a woman can engage in the act. Shifting should be carried out with the facial lips only – no other lips will be tolerated.'

Since the news, thousands of Irish couples have started openly shifting on the street, meeting widespread disapproval from the older generation.

'What will the church allow them to do next?' asked one irate churchgoer. 'This new Pope is too easy-going, if you ask me.'

The term shifting was first introduced by the church in 1967, after the word 'kiss' was banned by Pope Paul VI. It has been used in Ireland ever since.

ROGUE MILKMAN INTRODUCES 'LOW-FAT' OPTION

Friday, 3 July 1984

The Tramore community has been left confused and highly suspicious of milkman Brendan Delaney, following his decision to introduce something known as a 'low-fat' option.

As little is known about the chemical make-up of this bewildering 'healthy' alternative, residents in the Tramore area have begun speculating about the nature of the substance.

Locals have offered a number of possible explanations for its presence on the milk float, suggesting that it could be 'a government experiment', 'that foreign shite', 'the gays trying to turn us gay', 'the leftover milk the Dublin folk didn't want' and, most worryingly, 'Delaney's wife's breast milk'.

In an exclusive interview with WWN, Mr Delaney claimed that the low-fat option is all the rage in England and that it could help his customer to 'shift those pesky extra pounds'.

These claims reportedly enraged a number of local Tramore men who besieged Mr Delaney's house and beat him up. 'Losing weight is for women' was then scrawled across the walls of his house by the angry and insecure men.

COCAINE, PROSTITUTION & MURDER: HOW LINE DANCING CHANGED IRELAND IN THE 90s

Line dancing hit Ireland in the 90s in a huge way, sparking a hip-led sexual revolution. Now, for the first time ever, WWN can reveal the hidden darkness behind the sexiest form of dance ever to grace these shores.

'I'd say by 1994 my hip movement was verging on the pornographic,' line dancing instructor Cillian Higgins recalls. 'You have to remember that those were different times. I could have gone to jail if I had been caught teaching line dancing.'

Line dancing only became legal in Ireland in 1999, but by then the nation's appetite for the daring art form had all but dried up. Waterford native Conor Lyons is credited with being the first Irish man ever to line dance, in Arizona in the summer of 1989.

'My father beat the head off me when he found out. He said, "No son of mine is taking up the Devil's dance",' Lyons explained. But it wasn't long until word spread and an underground line dancing movement began.

Many people from the older generation were militantly pro-Irish dancing and took great exception to the new craze, with several dance-offs resulting in tragedy.

'I made several female Irish dancers, who I was in dance-offs with, collapse and faint when they witnessed the sheer sexual ferocity with which I danced the famously rigid and asexual dance,' Lyons admitted, breaking down in tears.

Local pimps soon became intrigued by Lyons and his magic hips, forcing him into sexual slavery, prostituting his hips out to lonely housewives all over the Midlands.

'I'm not necessarily proud of it, but yes, women did get untold pleasure out of my step two-four, step two-four. I was put on a diet of cocaine by my pimp, and in fairness, it helped loosen the hips after a long day.'

Rural communities were awash with line dancing activity, with many young people actively learning the dance and competing nationwide.

'You had these rooms and barns, dripping in sexual tension as people danced to Kenny Roger's "The Gambler". You won't find a more sexual song in my opinion,' Karen Gregory, a reformed line dancer, explained.

By 1997 the Gardaí had a dedicated Line Dancing Crackdown Squad, which patrolled the country, breaking up barn dances and arresting people. Something that had brought so

much illicit joy was now being slowly suffocated by the government.

'Well, I was arrested at a dance in Clare,' Lyons revealed, 'I was marched up to Dublin and forced to register my hips as deadly weapons. It was a truly dark time.'

Lyons was sentenced to ten years in prison, and forced to learn Irish dancing while in Mountjoy prison. He had attended his last hoedown throwdown.

By 1999 twenty thousand Irish people had been arrested for their participation in the line dancing phenomenon, but after pressure from several prominent American country musicians as well as an admission from Gay Byrne that he had line danced once, the government overturned their convictions, legalising the dance and setting the prisoners free.

'It's still tough thinking about those wild days, but I think we made Ireland a better place with our dancing,' Lyons concluded.

LIFESTYLE

No sexy singles in your area waiting to chat, finds independent enquiry

A new report, due tomorrow, is to reveal that – contrary to what may be suggested by late-night advertisements on television or side-bar ads on the internet – there are no sexy singles in your area waiting to chat to you.

The Sexy Singles Survey (SSS) was carried out by local authorities across Ireland and found that not only are there no sexy single girls near you, but also that your nearest sexy single girl may be up to fifty miles away.

'A lot of what you see advertised is grossly exaggerated,' claimed Dr Frank Murphy, chief census taker for the SSS. 'Claims that there are sexy singles just fifteen minutes away are wildly exaggerated. There are people in West Cork, the Burren, Malin Head ... their nearest sexy single could be a two-hour bus journey away. If you live on Valentia Island you'll need to get a ferry to meet the nearest sexy single, and you'll need to travel further if she won't agree to meet you at the port.'

The news comes as a heavy blow to the legions of lonely horndogs living in the more rural parts of Ireland, although Dr Murphy went on to assure the nation that, although your area may not have a grouping of sexy singles as close as you may want, there is light at the end of the tunnel.

'One thing we did discover is that there are certainly girls living in your area,' said Dr Murphy, as he clicked around on Facebook, 'although to call them sexy singles is a bit of a stretch. A lot of them aren't single, and a lot of them are in bits. Most of them don't want to talk to you, let alone chat or flirt. But rest assured; there are women near to where you are.'

Murphy was also quick to point out that his survey wasn't limited to sexy singles, and that there were also far fewer bored housewives, lonely MILFs, and cock-craving barely-legal sluts in your area than you may have been led to believe.

MOTORING NEWS

Dangerously close BMW just checking out your hilarious bumper sticker

The driver of a BMW who was inches away from your car was obviously just checking out your hilarious bumper sticker back there and not trying to force you into a slower lane of traffic.

Mark Dunne, the door-to-door insurance salesman behind you, was almost definitely chuckling away to himself at your fantastic wit, which forced him to flash his headlights repeatedly in hysterics.

His obvious appreciation was further cemented by a series of beeps from his 5-series car-horn and then animated through various different types of hand gestures that you somehow failed to understand.

Pulling into the slow lane to your left, Mr Dunne passed you on the inside in a bid to congratulate your genius with a rather stern but knowing stare, before flooring the car's 3-litre accelerator to the ground, leaving behind an air of camaraderie that can be only found on a busy Irish motorway.

Finally realising your rather average land speed, you veer off gently much to the delight of the rather large stream of traffic behind you, who will now certainly miss out on your most hilarious 'if you can read this, then you're too close' bumper sticker.

Eight-year-old won't shut the fuck up talking about Minecraft

A second class pupil at St David's National School, Joey Clancy, has not once stopped talking about the computer game Minecraft for almost twelve months, family, friends and teachers revealed today.

Clancy, aged 8¾, has developed the cunning ability to crowbar the 3-D procedurally generated world into every goddamn conversation he can, forcing his worried carers into action.

'When I get home from school, I'm going to build a pirate ship that shoots cannons and kill loads of creepers,' he told teacher Catherine Kennedy yesterday when she asked

him for his homework. 'Then I'm gonna put loads of zombies in the ship and blow it up with TNT.'

Following several warnings from the school about his behaviour, parents Kevin and Peggy Clancy were forced to limit their son's screen time. 'It has only made him worse,' Kevin Clancy told WWN. 'For instance, this morning, we found him building some sort of fort out

of all the cushions in the sitting room. He has even started walking weird and making chomping noises – like the characters in the game. We also found a large hole that he'd dug in the garden. He said it was to trap pig mobs. Like, what the hell is a mob? Joey said he wants to be an Enderman when he grows up. Seriously, he won't shut the fuck up talking about Minecraft.'

Worried for the welfare of their only son, the couple later confirmed that they will admit him to a local centre for addiction, where he will spend the next ten weeks in rehabilitation. 'It's for the best,' concluded his mother.

FUTUREWATCH

THE REINTRODUCTION OF THE SLOW SET

What would a future in which the sadly missed slow set of a disco was not only reintroduced but made mandatory look like? WWN takes a look into the crystal ball ...

1) STREET CRIME FIGURES PLUMMET

Without the slow set to blow off a week's worth of sexual frustration, our young people are currently spilling out of nightclubs and hitting the person nearest to them with the first bottle they see. Following the reintroduction of the slow set, all this aggression will boil off before they even get to the street.

2) ALCOHOL-RELATED INJURIES CEASE TO EXIST

As people spend more and more time locked at the pelvis while swaying to Bryan Adams and licking the inside of each others

heads, they simultaneously avoid drinking their faces off at the bar. A&E departments report a miraculous drop in stomach pumping and head injuries.

3) STDS AND UNWANTED PREGNANCIES FALL BY 95 PER CENT

As people get all the lovin' they need during five or six power ballads from the eighties, they feel less of an urge to just grab a randomer and sleep with them. People just kiss for twenty minutes on the dance floor, shake hands and then go home to their separate beds. Chlamydia vanishes in less than six weeks.

4) QUEUES FOR CHIPS SHORTEN BY HALF

Single people currently queue in the chip shop for their own post-club meals, but after the slow set becomes mandatory, queues are cut by half as the man stands in line for the kebabs while the lady waits outside, staring longingly at him as if he's just the greatest thing in the world.

5) SALES OF ROSES BY ROMANIANS SOAR

Romanians selling roses outside nightclubs finally make a sale as happy couples pour out into the night. Who wouldn't want to buy a rose for the lady? Only two euro? We'll take five!

'Won't be long now,' says old man, referring to nothing in particular

Greeting the other passengers as he boarded the bus at the stop outside his local post office, William Ferris, a 77-year-old retired teacher from Waterford, squinted slightly, stopping to assess who he was looking at before taking a deep breath. 'Won't be long now,' Ferris said while exhaling, much to the bemusement of those within earshot.

'What's that now?' Sarah Quinlan, a 26-year-old retail worker, asked politely as the old man's gaze landed on her. 'Ah yeah,' Ferris responded in an effort to clarify his earlier non-specific and open-ended comment.

'What won't be long now?' enquired Eileen Filan, who happened to be on a trip into town on the day of Ferris's remarks. Ferris then looked out of the window, smiling for a moment before adding, 'Lovely day for it.'

'Ah, no seriously, what the fuck are ya on about, fella?' entreated

Leo Sinclair, a local ruffian also on board who was apparently fed up with the obscure nature of Ferris's conversational gambits.

'Yeah, yeah, ah yeah,' Ferris concluded as he found himself a seat, with the small crowd none the wiser as to what exactly he was getting at.

The life of a Dublin teenager just got a whole lot more interesting. The inclusion of a stripe of blue in her otherwise mousey brown hair has doubled her levels of quirkiness, hopefully boosting her social standing at school.

Laura O'Whelan, 16, took the drastic steps after realising her Misfits T-shirt and love of Tim Burton movies weren't doing enough to cement her position as the kooky girl in her class.

With a strict ban on facial piercings and tattoos in place, O'Whelan decided to express her individuality through the medium of dyed hair, opting for Punk Chick Blue no. 7 from the limited range in her local pharmacy.

With the dyeing process deemed a complete success, the straight-A student is looking forward to

Teenager's life 100 per cent more interesting now she has put a blue stripe in her hair

parading her badass new look at the front of the Central Bank this weekend, where it will make her stand out among the other girls who opted for Punk Chick Blue no. 8 and Punk Chick Blue no. 9.

'It's my hair, so if you don't like it, then whatever,' said O'Whelan, despite really, really hoping that you like her hair. 'I'm not one of those pretty-girl types who fixate on how they dress and how they look. I'm

just more about expressing my style, which takes hours of planning. I mean, look at the blue streak in my hair; look at it! Okay, why are you looking at my hair? Have you never seen someone with a blue streak before? Get over yourself.'

O'Whelan is expected to keep the blue streak in her hair until at least Monday next week, at which point she will change it to a pink stripe because ... you wouldn't understand.

EXCLUSIVE

Children running around playground will 'sleep tonight' claims grandmother

A County Waterford grandmother has predicted that her daughter's three children 'will sleep tonight' after bringing them to a local park to play in the hot summer sun.

It was confirmed that Tracey Hunt made the comments to another woman she didn't actually know, who also seemed to be supervising kids of her own.

'I was just there, minding my own business, when this elderly lady sat down and started making assumptions about her grandchildren's future sleeping patterns,' explained Anne

Hennebry. 'It was quite strange as she suggested the children would all sleep tonight. Including my own. It seemed like a weird thing to say, considering the majority of children these days sleep at night. I wasn't sure if there was something sinister about her statement, or if it was a threat, so I called the local Gardaí.'

Worried for the safety of the children, Gardaí arrived on the

scene with two members of the Department of Social and Family Affairs to question the woman, and take the children into care.

'They were very upset about being split up from their grandmother, but we had to make sure she wasn't going to kill them later that night,' said Garda Tadgh Moore.

Following several hours of questioning, Gardaí later released the 67-year-old, stating they believed that her motives were innocent, and that she did not plan on putting the children to sleep forever.

5 Ways to cope with a baby who won't pose for cute Facebook photos

Babies! Children! Offspring! Not only can they be a vital well of much-needed organs in later life, they're also one of the foremost sources of social media gratification available! Post a cute pic of your kid being cute and watch those likes roll in!

But what if your infant won't get with the programme? Sometimes children are too young to realise the value of a retweet, and will steadfastly refuse to turn their stupid cute faces to the camera. Here's 5 tips for any parent out there who wants those sweet notifications to start coming!

1) Be patient

No matter how many times you repeat your child's name, they'll just keep playing, and learning, and developing their motor skills, all while ignoring you! So it's important to just wait ... always have your phone or camera at the ready for when they turn and hit that perfect pose. In many ways, taking the perfect snap of a toddler has less in common with true photography, and more in common with, say, hunting a deer with a bow and arrow.

2) Snap everything

Sometimes, you just have to play the odds. Your kid may never stare down the lens with that cherubic look on their face that your sister's kids have in her Facebook posts, so you'll just have to up your coverage. Start taking pictures of your baby at dawn, and just continue to do so throughout the day. Scour the images at night to find something that you could post on Instagram without looking like a bad parent. Sure, the kid might only smile when he's licking something he picked out of the bin, but if it means a cute picture, you can crop the garbage out later!

3) Use the same picture over and over

Kids are easier to photograph when they're smaller, before their little minds develop and they want to do something other than pose for a relentless barrage of Facebook profilers. So if you have a treasured picture of them when they were small, simply use Paint to crop them out of that, and paste them into new shots! People may ask why the kid appears to not be ageing as the months turn into years, but you can just ignore them. Alternatively, just circle the baby's face and paste that on to shots of them as they grow up, like some sort of ghoulish baby-face mask.

4) Use someone else's kids

If your ungrateful asshole baby won't pose cutely for you, then find one that will. In a shopping centre, on the street, on the bus ... if you see a cute kid, just quickly sidle up to them and take a sneaky selfie. People won't notice that you're tagging yourself in pictures with an increasingly disparate group of infants – nobody really looks at these things anyway.

5) Draw a face on your knee

This one is so foolproof, you don't even need an actual child! Simply hug your knee close to your chest, and draw a face on it. Drape a blanket around it, and selfie away to your hearts content! 'Just snuggling up to my baby', 'Me and my baby watching some TV LOL'... You can post a full range of social media staples while your own kid does whatever the hell he wants elsewhere in the house. #SOCUTE!

Mother-of-three ready to quit after just three hours of Easter holidays

Nuala Purcell, a loving and dedicated mother to three beautiful children – Niall (11), Sinead (9) and Coman (4) – has admitted that she is ready to quit, change her identity and move abroad after just three hours in their company.

Although Nuala has claimed on at least 4,132 separate occasions that her children are 'her everything', she was sorely tested within the first three hours of having them all in the house together this morning. 'I'm not a bad mother, but a life in Hawaii as a hula girl doesn't sound so bad. I'd even take a job as a Colombian drug mule at this stage,' she told WWN.

While Nuala has previously confirmed to many friends that she was indeed 'born to be a mother', the mum-of-three has now dramatically retracted that statement. 'I'm born to be a mother for a maximum of nine hours a day: without school to drop them off at, I'm cracking,' Nuala added.

With Easter camps not an option for Nuala – as they cost an arm and a leg as well as hundreds of euro – the loving mother has been left with few options.

Nuala had alerted her children to the presence of the outdoors, and informed them of the possibility of fun trips to the park, but Niall, Sinead and Coman immediately vetoed these ideas with repeated and targeted screaming.

'I've tried to reason with them but they always come back to me with a "why?" so I'm locking myself in my room and listening to my "Sounds of the Ocean" CD on repeat,' Nuala added, with a distinct lack of hope in her voice.

Nuala then took to looking up cheap flights out of the country and daydreaming about her husband meeting another woman with the patience of a saint who would happily look after her three demonic children.

New ginger emojis to be used primarily to bully gingers

Celebrations by the world's ginger community upon securing new ginger emojis were curtailed by millions of bullies pointing out that they will use the emojis as a bullying aide.

'Ha ha, look at the big ginger head on this one,' self-confessed bully Martin Dowling (53) said, pointing at one particular ginger emoji before sending it immediately to his ginger friend, coupled with a witty put-down along the lines of 'ginger prick'.

Ginger rights, the last great civil rights movement of our times, have come into focus in recent years due to people's predisposition to pass remarks about anyone carrying the ginger gene.

While the strawberry blonde faction maintains that this is not their fight as they are 'totally not ginger', a small band of diehard gingers continues to campaign for change.

'I was sick of every ginger on TV and in movies playing the token ginger. Why couldn't they be the guy that got the girl, or the hero?' explained Ginger 'Til I Die campaigner Barry Kinsella. 'The release of these new ginger emojis is the first step as our ginger sensitivity workshops were unsuccessful.'

Swyft Media created the set of emojis but hadn't planned for their use as fodder for bullies with nothing better to do.

'We've heard of one man receiving a Whatsapp message with a ginger emoji next to a clenched fist emoji. The shocking implications are clear. The sender has a real intent to pummel the recipient out of existence,' Swyft spokesman Dan Finn told WWN.

This latest episode reveals that gingers still have a long way to travel to get to the road less discriminated. Ginger 'Til I Die has launched a new fruitless appeal for gingers to be called redheads instead.

WEATHER NEWS

Neighbour can't believe the weather we're having

The neighbour down the road is finding it difficult to believe the weather we're having today, it has been revealed.

Margaret Holden, who's married to John, said it was like summer out there now, and that she was sorry she had put on her coat before leaving the house. 'I'm beat with the heat,' she said, as she passed several people outside a

shop. 'I can't believe the weather we're having.'

Following Mrs Holden's comments, concerned family members brought the 64-year-old to hospital, where she was diagnosed with acute psychosis, before being transferred to Saint Oteran's mental health facility in Waterford.

'She just couldn't believe the weather so we figured she may be having problems with reality in general,' son Mark told WWN. 'Last week she couldn't believe what time it was when I told her, and my sister Kate said Mam could have sworn Friday was Saturday.'

The grandmother-of-ten will have a full frontal lobotomy later this afternoon and is expected to remain in care for the rest of her days. 'I think we did the right thing here,' added her son. 'She wouldn't want to put the family out.'

MUSIC NEWS

Great new song ruined now that your mother is humming it

That song you've been singing for the last month is now completely ruined after you found your mother humming the living daylights out of it earlier this afternoon while she was doing some ironing.

Completely unaware she had access to Spin 103.8, you realised the gravity of the situation when you found her humming 'FourFiveSeconds' by Rihanna, Kanye West and Paul McCartney.

It is thought you will be close to vomiting by the time your mother gets around to singing the line 'I might get a little drunk' before letting out an excited and playful giggle.

Despite your protestations, your mother will explain, 'I know Paul McCartney very well. He's been going since I was a child; and did you know he wrote the greatest song of all time – "Mull of Kintyre"?'

It is thought that the combined pop culture credentials of Rihanna and Kanye West will not be enough to save your favourite song of the moment from being ruined as you permanently link it to the memory of your mother trying to dance with you while saying 'What? I'm cool!'

Twenty-five per cent of all cutting-edge chart music suffers the indignity of being enjoyed by parents up and down the country. You can spot these singles by a sharp rise in CD sales but a dramatic drop in YouTube and Spotify streaming.

Collecting yourself momentarily, you had convinced yourself that the song could retain some of its magic – until your mother asked, 'What does wildin' mean?'

According to recent research, WWN can reveal that over 450,000 songs in the last decade have fallen victim to the dreaded parental endorsement.

Small-town clique of sessioners running out of friends to sleep with

A local clique of sessioners who have spent the majority of their lives living in each other's pockets are slowly running out of friends to sleep with, sources inside the group have concluded this week.

The Clonmel town posse found themselves coming full-circle at the weekend after attending the Body and Soul festival in Ballinlough Castle, County Westmeath.

'Jamie ended up going off with Ciara again for the twentieth time since they split in 2001,' long-time member of the clique Gerry Hackett told WWN. 'I think everyone has gone off with everyone else at this stage.'

'This whole going-out-with-the-same-bunch-of-people-for-fifteen-years thing is starting to get old if I'm honest. There's only so many more house parties and festivals I can bear. We're all hitting our thirties now like.'

As with many small-town cliques of their generation, the Elm Park contingent have been together for longer than humanly expected, with many outsiders stating that the whole thing is starting to look a bit creepy.

'I used to hang around all the lads briefly when I left school,' explained Tommy Hayes, who fell out with the faction after being wrongly accused of stealing a bag of speckled doves from Ken, who actually lost them in a Portaloo at Creamfields 2000. 'Then I grew up and realised spending time with large groups of people who took drugs all weekend and slept around with each other wasn't healthy, but actually counterproductive to living a fruitful and successful life.'

Realising their looping nature, several members of the clique vowed to take a break from going out with each other for a while, at least until Martin's birthday BBQ bash in July, which is going to be epic as Dermot is getting a book of trips and some base speed from a lad in Cork he knows through Declan Twomey, who left the group to find work but keeps in contact because he's still in love with Deirdre who's engaged to everyone's best friend, Skinny Welsh.

ww news

Waterford Whispers News

HOROSCOPES

Libra

23 September–22 October

This week Libra is on holidays.

Scorpio

23 October–21 November

Your death goes unnoticed.

Sagittarius

22 November–21 December

You send your sex life into new and exciting places by masturbating with your left hand.

Aries

21 March–19 April

Switching to a Palaeolithic, gluten-free, non-dairy diet will temporarily give a sense of purpose to your otherwise shallow and meaningless life.

Taurus

20 April–20 May

Take a chance and ask out that girl who's on your train every morning! Statistics show that women find being chatted up while commuting creepy and off-putting, but it'll be a laugh for the rest of us.

Gemini

21 May –20 June

OMG! You will hear a song on the radio that was TOTALLY written about you. It's eerie. It's like they know you. They know your soul.

Cancer

21 June–22 July

Those ideas that you've been working on for ages, the ones that you really feel could propel you to the next level in your career? Better keep them to yourself. What if everyone thinks they're stupid? Don't kid yourself that you can handle that kind of rejection.

Leo

23 July–22 August

Having binge-watched those four leaked episodes of *Game Of Thrones*, you now have nothing to watch for the next month. Well done, genius. Real good work.

Virgo

23 August–22 September

Fuck it, update Adobe Flash. What's the worst that could happen?

Capricorn

22 December–19 January

You will start to compare yourself unfavourably with Jennifer Lawrence.

Aquarius

20 January–18 February

'The pen is mightier than the sword' proves to be utter bullshit when you're challenged to a duel by an eighteenth-century French aristocrat later this week.

Pisces

19 February–20 March

This week you will mostly be a disappointment to yourself ... Oh, you don't like what I have to say? Fine. Go buy a fucking fortune cookie, you ungrateful prick!

Culchie girl develops D4 accent in record time

A Tipperary teenager has smashed the world record for developing a D4 accent, which she acquired after spending less than a week on work placement in a Dublin office.

It took Saoirse Moffatt, 19, just four days to morph her broad Thurles brogue into a voice with hints of a Dublin accent, and another twelve hours before she developed a completely convincing southside twang.

The transformation from culchie cadence to affluent accent takes the average teenage girl at least a semester of college, although some have managed it in a little over a month. Moffatt's ability to change her voice in less than a week shattered the record, with many wondering if she will ever be beaten.

'To her credit, Saoirse started to change the way she talked almost straight away,' said Hope Devereux, HR manager at the accountancy firm where Ms Moffat was on a work placement from Carlow IT.

'It's almost like she spotted our smirks when we first heard her speak, and got to work on trying to sound like us. Her eights, greats, plates and lates were the first to change; and then there was a significant alteration to the words and phrases she used. In less than a day, she was saying 'Oh my God' instead of 'Oh be the Jaysus'; the day after that, you'd swear she'd lived her whole life in Terenure.'

Ms Moffatt is expected to retain her new accent until she returns to Thurles this weekend, at which point her friends and family will laugh it out of her.

Dublin girl doesn't care what she gets for Christmas as long as it's expensive

Dublin girl Emer O'Reilly isn't all that fussed when it comes to Christmas, WWN can exclusively reveal.

While out in trendy new haunt The Bushman's Kangaroo, Emer and friends were busy discussing their manic plans for the holiday season over some linner, which is totally the new brunch.

'All these ads have just, like, warped people's brains,' confessed a concerned Emer to friends. 'Like you'd think the world was ending the way people are running about, it's like re-fucking-lax.'

Emer was at pains to state that Christmas has, in recent years, got out of hand with too much pressure to get the right gifts.

'Like I was thinking the other day, I've had to get my mom to give me €100 for my dad's present, and ask my dad for €100 for my mom's present. That's only because of all the talk from the girls about what they're buying their folks. Christmas has gone completely over the top,' the 26-year-old accountant explained to her friends while failing to mention the fact that €70 of the money for her mother's gift would be spent on Emer's cut and blow dry the next day.

As linner continued into its third course and fourth cocktail, the mood amongst Emer and her friends soured further as they struggled with expectations for their own presents.

'Look, I think we've all heard how demanding Siobhan can be with her parents, but I'm not going into a complete bitch mode like her. I'm not picky as long as it's comfortably worth over a thousand euro,' Emer informed friends.

'New York was great, but I know he got the tickets on the cheap in an Aer Lingus sale,' Emer added, as she discussed the present she received from her bus driver father last year. 'You'd just hope he doesn't lose the run of himself and spend all the money on getting my mom something too expensive 'cause she won't bloody appreciate it, the ungrateful cow.'

Waterford man still sending Farmville requests

Friends and family of Waterford man Tom Carroll have expressed their concern after observing that the 43-year-old is still sending Farmville requests on Facebook, some years after the practice became unfashionable on the social network site.

The 43-year-old, seemingly unaware that the rest of the world has moved on, constantly bombards his social circle with incessant pleading for gifts which would help him progress in a game long forgotten by modern civilisation.

'I mean, Jesus, Middle Eastern dictators have risen to power and then been overthrown again in the last few years; we've had the iPhone 6, the Apple Watch, the 2012 Olympics and this prick is still all about fucking Farmville,' concerned friend Charlie Cummings revealed to WWN.

' "Tom Carroll has sent you a haystack for your farm in Farmville. Could you help him by sending something back?" I can in my hoop – I thought they took Farmville out by the shed and put a bullet in its head,' Cummings added.

Concern was palpable for Carroll at a recent family barbecue, when relations and friends gathered to try and wean him off the prehistoric social media time waster in favour of more current games such as Candy Crush.

'Candy Crush is already well past its sell-by date, but I thought "baby steps", you know?' Carroll's wife Joanne explained. 'But his eyes just glazed over. The next day everyone had fresh bloody requests. It's ... it's ... it's tearing us apart.'

Carroll, for his part, seems completely unaware that his requests are slowly making him a Facebook and a real-life pariah.

'I've spent about €5,000 of Farm Cash within the game, and, Jesus, I'm flying. I'm the envy of all the guys on my friends list. They keep trying to put me off it because I'm king of the Farmville castle, boi!' Carroll concluded.

Rescue team attempts to free man trapped in the nineties

A team of highly trained rescue staff, specialising in helping people who are trapped in the past, is currently attempting to free a Wexford man who is unable to get out of the 90s

The squad, comprising a hair and fashion expert as well as music and film buffs will attempt to drag Enniscorthy native Martin Carolan into the current decade – a task which they say will require weeks of delicate work.

Carolan, 37, has been trapped in the 90s since the year 2000, having failed to move on with all of his friends as they embraced the culture and experiences of the new millennium.

The 37-year-old steadfastly stuck with the hairstyles and clothing that he had chosen in the 90s, and still counts Eminem and Oasis as his favourite recording artists, listening to '(What's the Story) Morning Glory?' at least twice a week.

Carolan's friends made the distress call to the rescuers, in the hope that they will be able to free him from the decade he's stuck in.

'He's missing out on so much, sitting at home in his mam's house, listening to Britpop and watching *The Matrix*,' said Ian Harding, long-time friend of the trapped man.

'This rescue squad should be able to give him a haircut that doesn't make him look like Brett Anderson, as well as some clothes other than Ben Sherman shirts. Hopefully this time next week he'll have been brought up to date. If he'd at least buy an Eminem album that was released after *The Marshall Mathers LP*, it'd be a start.'

The team will attempt the rescue in a slow, methodical manner, amid fears that rushing could result in a collapse of Nokia chargers and half empty bottles of CK One.

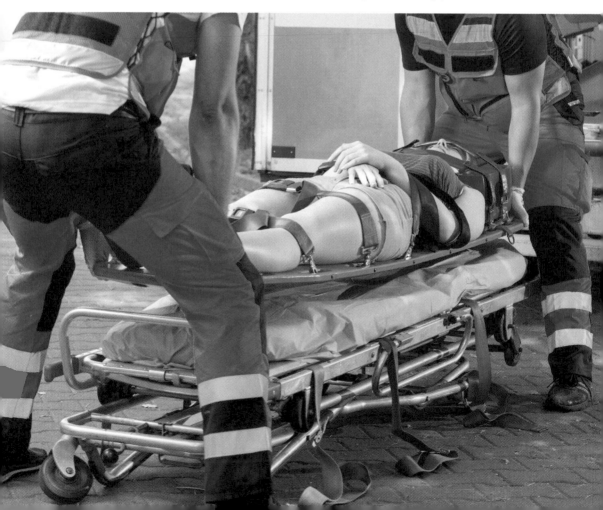

5 ways to know if your curves are the good curves or the bad curves

Ladies! With summer upon us, many of you are getting ready to show off your beach bodies, after hiding them away from us like the selfish little minxes you are.

But how can you be sure that your body is the kind of body we even want to see? Sure, you may be happy with the way you look, but what has your opinion ever counted for? This season is all about curves, but how can you tell if your curves are the good curves or the bad curves? Follow our 5-step curve identification programme to see what celebrity you most resemble, and use it as a guide as to whether you should hit the beach like a goddess, or hide your foul carcass in the mines for the rest of your miserable life.

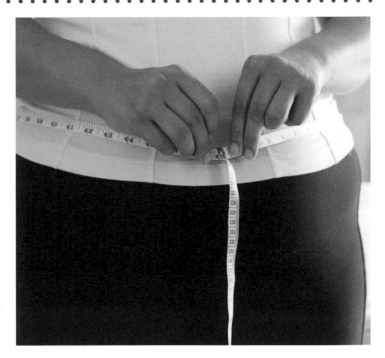

1) Keira Knightley

WOW! Check out the curves on Keira! Adding lean athletic muscle to her naturally slender frame, she looks hideous! But how about those curves? Truly they are the kind of curves that all women should be jealous of, and if you're lucky enough to look like this, then go eat some cake. You disgust us. Nobody wants to see you looking like this.

2) Kelly Brook

Kelly Brook has always wowed the sands with her stunning curves, which are a disgrace and should remain covered up. We all like curves, but there's curves and then there's curves. Kelly Brook's fabulous curves? Unacceptable.

3) Kate Upton

To the lay person, one might say that Kate Upton and Kelly Brook share the same curvy figures, but the expert eye is able to spot key differences. One has a body to die for, the other is a hideous mess. We're not even sure which is which. There is such a fine margin of error when it comes to curves, ladies. A quarter of an inch too curvy? You're a fat pig. A quarter of an inch not curvy enough? Which eating disorder is it this week, precious?

4) Helen Mirren

WOW. That is all we can say. These are curves that would be the envy of a woman half her age. We hope we look as good as the gorgeous Helen Mirren does when we're 69. If we do, we will kill ourselves in disgust for allowing ourselves to be seen in public like this. She looks wretched. Hit the gym, old timer!

5) Suri Cruise

Looking as cute as a button, Suri Cruise looked fucking awful when she hit the beach earlier this week. The pretty 9-year-old may have thought she could escape beach body scrutiny, but she was sorely mistaken – someone will always be watching, always be judging! Sorry, ladies, it comes with the vagina!

To make sure you don't make the same mistakes as our horrendous, beautiful celebrities, get yourself to the gym to work off those curves, while adding other curves to the curves you already have. Curve your curves into curves, but make sure you don't over-curve your other curves. We'll let you know if you're doing it right!

Ancient cave painting shows man struggling to assemble IKEA furniture

A group of archaeologists – led by TCD historian and archaeologist Breffny O'Dalaigh – has made a 'one-of-a-kind' discovery of ancient cave drawings which illustrate the difficulties that even primitive man had with assembling IKEA flat-pack furniture.

'It was truly humbling to find them,' O'Dalaigh revealed to WWN, 'and to know that we were probably the first people to see them for millennia. It is this kind of universal thread that links us back to our ancestors

who clearly fucking hated putting together IKEA furniture as much as we do today.'

Prominent archaeologists worldwide have marvelled at the astonishing detail of the drawings, which

provides a valuable insight into how humans coped with their daily tasks all those years ago.

'My favourite one shows a woman pointing angrily at the instructions, with the man shrugging his shoulders, unable to explain why there are four screws left,' O'Dalaigh added, beaming from cheek to cheek.

Frustrated furniture-haters the world over have voiced their disappointment, however, at the news that the drawings provide no quick-fix solutions to a problem that has plagued mankind since time immemorial.

'So they just half-read the instructions and then ploughed on until there wasn't a piece to spare, like we do now? Yeah, eh, thanks for the insight there, cave lads,' remarked serial IKEA-furniture-destroyer Ian Gardiner.

Man makes zero sense while describing epic dream he had

An excited Galway man has found himself quite unable to put into words the exact events of an epic dream he had, but has assured those around him that it was 'mad shit altogether'.

Sean White, 27, struggled to describe the dream to his wife and his co-workers today, despite it being one of the most vivid

nocturnal experiences of his life. Attempts to explain just what made it so brilliant have resulted in the Oranmore native drifting off into tales which lack both coherence and reason.

'It had ... it was in this place, sorta like here but not really ... and my da was there, and my old metalwork teacher,' said White, trying to convey

the key points of the dream to his co-workers at the local iron smelting plant. 'But then it all changed, and I was ... not flying – more like I could time my jumps so that I didn't land on the ground, do you know what I mean? 'Twas mental.'

White's position is one shared by many people across the country, who wake from vivid dreams, be they enjoyable or terrifying, and feel the need to describe them to those around them.

Almost every time, the dreamer will be unable to put into words just what made the dream so interesting and exciting, and will also fail to spot the signs that the person they are talking to really doesn't give a shit.

The heartwarming moment an Irish lad fucks off to Australia

A video that shows the heartwarming moment a young Irish lad finally left for Australia has gone viral, after being posted on social media by his sister.

Cathal McCarron, described by close members of his family as a total prick, left to catch his flight to Perth this morning after years of living at home, scrounging off his parents and getting wasted every day.

McCarron, 23, made the decision to leave for Australia after hearing reports from his friends that it was 'some craic altogether', prompting him to continue paying no rent or upkeep to his mother in a bid to save up enough dole to get a ticket. Having failed to accrue enough cash to take him to Oz, McCarron's parents gladly gave him the price of the airfare, in a last-ditch attempt to get him the fuck out of the house.

Sheila McCarron, his 18-year-old sister, recorded the look of relief

on her mother's face this morning as her brother finally left, before posting it on her Facebook page under the heading 'at fucking last'.

'I didn't expect it to go so viral' said Sheila, speaking about the 1:35 clip which has been watched over 300,000 times.

'I guess it just was something different, unlike all the clips people post of people coming home from abroad and getting loads of hugs and kisses and the like. We're not sad to see the back of Cathal, in fact, no one in town is. Australia is welcome to him.'

WWN Guide to
Ruining
Movember
for Everyone

Although the basic idea of Movember – grow a 'sponsored moustache' throughout November in a bid to raise money and awareness for prostate cancer research – is a noble one, it doesn't always help individuals draw enough attention to themselves.

So if you want to get involved in Movember without worrying that you won't get the credit you deserve, then simply follow WWN's easy guide!

1) Just grow a beard and shave it with two days to go

The rules of Movember are simple; you start off clean-shaven on the 1st of the month, cultivating a comical 'tache over the next thirty days. But that may leave you looking foolish for a full month! Take the simpler option and just grow a beard, then shave it into a moustache on 28 November. Some may say this is cheating, but what do you care?

2) Take constant selfies

Raising money for charity doesn't benefit you if you don't make it your business to fill up people's social media timelines with hourly selfies, charting the growth of your mo. Use captions such as 'LOL – what do I look like?!' and 'OMG! State of me!' to hopefully draw flattering comments about how you're actually looking pretty good.

3) Elevate the situation

Ok, so you're growing a moustache; so is everyone during Movember! You don't stand out! Rectify this by knocking everything up a notch or two. Dye your facial hair green! Put beads in it! Sculpt it into elaborate shapes. Don't let the attention slip away from you for even a minute!

4) Just never shut the fuck up about it

Be sure to mention your participation in Movember to everyone you meet, as they may not be able to correlate the moustache on your face with what month it is. Be sure to use the phrase 'Movember' as many times as humanly possible throughout the month, until the sound of it no longer inspires people to donate money to cancer charities, and instead makes them just think of hipster shitebags who love themselves.

special
feature

Bickering kids know Dad has no notion of actually turning the car around

A trio of young boys have decided to continue fighting and yelling at each other on a road trip with their parents, having worked out that their father's threats to 'turn this car around and go home' are unlikely to be carried out.

Sean Henighan, 7, along with his brothers Michael, 5, and Liam, 3, have been acting up since they left their home in Kilkenny this morning for a trip to Dublin Zoo.

Despite constant warnings from their father, Jim – who claims if the boys don't settle down then they'll all just go home and nobody will get to go to the zoo – the boys have opted to keep up the misbehaving, as historically these threats have never been followed through.

The kids cited previous journeys – such as last summer's trip to Trabolgan, during which they never stopped yelling the whole way – as proof that their father was bluffing when it came to threats made during road trips.

'We've weighed up the odds of Dad actually stopping the car and going home and we've decided that there's no way it's going to happen,' said Sean, acting as spokesperson for the children.

'We're more than halfway to Dublin, so it's easier for us to keep going than to turn back. Plus Dad would be in serious trouble with Mam if he didn't bring us to the zoo like he promised. So when you add it all up, we can be as loud and cheeky as we want with no fear.'

Sean went on to state that the boys were unlikely to behave themselves on the way home either, as their father would no longer have the 'I'll turn this car around and go home' card to play.

EXCLUSIVE

Golden retriever 'horrified' after stock image appears on Pedigree Chum cans

A golden retriever from the Midlands who sold his image rights to a stock photography company has expressed his disgust at the realisation that his image was being used to advertise Pedigree Chum.

Bouncer – 7 in human years, 49 in dog – posed for the images over three years ago as part of a series on dogs in Ireland. The photographs were then purchased in bulk by an online image library, and Bouncer signed away his rights, receiving no payment except a prolonged session of belly tickles.

The Athlone-based pet of two thought nothing more about the photos until it was brought to his attention earlier this week that his image was being used to advertise Pedigree Chum – and that he appeared on every can and bag of the popular dog food on shelves across the country.

'I would rather eat my own poop than Pedigree Chum,' said Bouncer, while eating his own poop. 'Perhaps I was naive when I signed away the rights to my image, but I guess I just thought that the photographs would never be picked for anything. I've talked to my lawyer, but it looks like I can't do much. I just hope this is a lesson to other dogs out there.'

In a clever PR move, Midlands animal feed firm Red Mills has approached Bouncer to appear as the poster canine for their own brand of dog food in their latest campaign.

Lo♥in' WATERFORD

launch edition

THE ONE AMAZING DISH ANY STUPID BOLLOCKS CAN MAKE

We know you all love the amazeballs recipes we post, but some of you have complained that our dishes are too hard to make. Like, whatever.

So today we're going to take you through the absolute simplest recipe of all time: chicken katsu sushi rolls. This is only one of the most delicious forms of sushi you've ever eaten, and as for easy? If you can tie your laces, you can manage this. Let's fucking cook!

1. Slice up two skinless chicken breasts into thin slices. Boom. Done.

2. Prepare a delicate Tempura batter using whatever method you feel like – just whichever way you normally like it. This will be crumbled later on and used to coat the outside of the katsu roll. Handy.

3. Fry your chicken in a coating of flour, egg and Japanese panko. Fire up that cast iron skillet to juuust the right temperature and fry that chicken until it's juuust cooked enough. You'll know when. Simps.

4. The roll we're doing here is a half-futomaki, so get your rice, get your romaine lettuce, get your chicken, and get your nori. You know what to do from here.

5. Get your makisu into action to help cover your roll in the tempura crumbs. BOSH. And you were going to get a takeaway for dinner. Idiot.

6. What the fuck are you waiting for? Eel sauce on that bitch, right now. Do it.

7. Kick back, fire up a documentary about something on Netflix, and get that tasty beast in your belly, A to the SAP. So fucking easy.

10 SNEAKY WAYS TO GRAB A DRINK ON GOOD FRIDAY

In our latest instalment of *Lo♥in'* **WATERFORD**, we bring you the essential guide to avoiding that slow-creeping feeling that you may be an alcoholic by laughing in the face of Ireland's archaic Intoxicating Liquor Act. Forgot to pick up some booze before the Good Friday lockdown? Read on for our solutions.

1) Own a car? Well rev that bad boy up and aim it at the nearest off-licence shutters – they look sturdier than they actually are. Once you've gained access to the premises it's time to prove your friends wrong; you don't have a drinking problem, you have a drinking solution. LOL!

2) No alcohol in the house? Well don't sit there beating yourself up. Instead visit your ailing grandmother or elderly aunt. Then, while they talk shite about how they're afraid of dying, raid their supply of gin, which is usually plentiful enough to last well into 2044.

3) Go to Mass! Traditionally the shitest wine in the history of mankind, it's best to wait until it has been turned into the blood of Christ, then after a quick Sign of the Cross grab the chalice and leg it. Downside to this one is that it's only good for a single glass.

4) We definitely put this next one into the 'only if you're desperate' category. The homeless seem to have secret pockets where they keep endless supplies of alcohol. Befriend a homeless person or, better yet, wrestle whatever drink they have out of their hands. They don't need it as much as you do.

5) If you're not keen on trashing your car by driving into an off-licence, you can always kidnap the proprietor's family at knifepoint and demand that he retrieve your special list of preferred beverages. This one is not for the faint-hearted, nor those who are afraid of spilling a little blood to show that they mean business.

6) This is probably the most obvious one on the list, but everyone knows a bored housewife who is in the throes of a cataclysmic slide into alcoholism, so if you can bear to listen to inane chitchat then this might be the solution for you. Just make sure you can stomach Lidl-brand red wine!

7) If you're a pro at this you'll only just be sobering up from last night's escapades so panic has yet to set in. Head to your nearest Tesco and seduce the security guard with your animal magnetism. Once you have agreed to marry him and provide him with several heirs to his security guard empire, you're just one nod and a wank away from getting into that locked-away booze.

8) Trains! What, you didn't know that you could legally purchase alcohol on trains if you're dressed as a train? A demeaning but necessary step towards that Good Friday booze session.

9) Got time on your hands? Why not break into your nearest pub and, instead of simply stealing from it, reset all the clocks so that you can prop up the bar and party like it's midnight from about 7 p.m. Don't start the party too early, though, or people might think you're desperate.

10) Attend a Narcotics Anonymous meeting. The folks there are usually making the transition to the harmless stopgap solution that is alcohol and should have plenty on their person, ensuring you can really enjoy your Good Friday without having it ruined by the inconvenience of sobriety.

4 MEALS THAT BARELY FILLED ME BUT WILL LOOK GREAT ON INSTAGRAM

What so many people seem to forget about food is that nutritional value and taste are almost meaningless compared to the overall power of a good Instagram photo.

We here at *Lo♥in'* **WATERFORD** can't tell you the number of times we've eaten a truly beautiful meal with amazing company, only to find that the Instagram pics just didn't gain traction, rendering the whole meal pointless.

So in order to make eating out a pleasurable social media experience, here are a few meals that, although they will barely fill you, will look a-maz-ing with whatever filter you choose!

1. Microscopic sweet potato & halloumi salad: it's just like a regular salad, but smaller! Technically it only feeds .0024 of a person, but it will look so cute and totally to-die-for next to your hands and cutlery. Bring your own microscope to ZoomFood on the quays.

2. Waterford eatery The Budgie Smugglers is the place to go for upscale, up-itself culinary wank, so naturally you need to get yourself down there to take as many pics of you and your crazy innovative meal as possible. Although the menu consists mainly of pulled pork, which is – let's face it – so passé now, the plates and cutlery are all hand-knitted by the residents of Corrofin Nursing Home in Galway. So although you'll still be starving and out of pocket, it'll totally be worth it when friends on social media see that you've got a knitted plate!

3. Haven't eaten in new hot spot The BourgeoiGee yet? You're really missing out. I went there three weeks before it was even open because that's how ahead of the curve we are here at *Lo♥in'* **WATERFORD**. Spanish artist Nával Gazé is the head chef and is constantly changing the menu, which we actually call curating now, because it sounds cooler. This week Gazé is playing music to water, infusing it with artistic intent. Snap a picture of that water next to the unique décor, which is mostly old vinyl records, and you've got yourself some serious re-grams. Note: it's probably worth eating before you go.

4. Ever wondered if it was possible to recreate great meals of the past? Well at Foodgasm, head chef Lionel Gack invites you to tell him the story of your greatest chipper experience. Give Lionel as much detail as possible and for the reasonable price of €50 he will carve out a single chip which is representative of that meal you are so desperate to recreate. Explain how high concept that is via a series of Instagram hashtags and you are guaranteed to be the envy of people who you really shouldn't be so desperate to impress in the first place!

4 EPIC PLACES TO DRINK CANS IN THE SUN

Hashtag sunshine! Following six consecutive hours of sunshine, we can officially announce the start of summer, and you know what that means ... major can drinkage!

We've compiled an epic list of epic places for you and your epic mates to drink epic cans in the epic sunshine until you're epically drunk, you big epic. Get your best skin top on, we're off for some can banter, AKA canter! HASHTAG CANTS!

1) BALLYBEG

Nowhere beats the Beg when it comes to epic canning in the sunshine! We spent most of the day enjoying a plastic bag full of cans in the scorching weather, taking in the sights, sounds, and smells of the area while cracking-looking young girls of indeterminate ages wandered past us wearing next to nothing. Cans, sunshine and hot chicks together in one place? That can only add up to one thing in Ballybeg: lads kicking the heads off each other while someone cries their eyes out and yells at them to stop.

2) BALLYBRICKEN

Ballybricken offers so much to the thirsty individual who just wants to sit on a bandstand and get his can on. While other venues only cater for fairweather drinkers, the BBK caters to those who wish to can it at any time of the year, or day, and as such attracts a more discerning class of can champion! Strictly cheap alcohol, though – don't come around here if you're drinking a recognised brand of lager or cider, you posh fuck!

3) THE PEOPLE'S PARK

For those who are new to the whole drinking game (and we're looking at you, middle-class teenage hipster LOL) there's The People's Park, which caters for everyone, from teenage girls with too much eye make-up to lads with red-and-black check shirts that have never actually been worn tied around their waists. Rough it up with your homies by lying on a blanket you borrowed from home while drinking a can of Miller with a slice of lemon in it. Don't get too drunk though – your mam won't like it when she comes to pick you up!

4) THE ARD RÍ

If what you're looking for is a conveniently located, abandoned hotel in which to enjoy a few cans while fearing for your life, look no further than the Ard Rí Hotel. With that much sought-after ambience of dread, the Ard Rí is the number one place to can it up when everywhere else in town is too packed, or too noisy, or just feels too safe. Overlooking the city, you can sit back and enjoy the beautiful sight of Waterford bathed in sunshine, blissfully blocking out the horrors housed in the decaying building. Also, free accommodation if you pass out! BONUS!